Spinnaker

R 'Bunty' King

SAIL BOOKS
34 Commercial Wharf
Boston, Massachusetts

For Wendy,
in the hope that
it will allay her fear of spinnakers

Copyright © R R King 1981

ISBN 0–914814–30–3

Printed in Great Britain by Fakenham Press Limited, Fakenham, Norfolk

This edition published in 1981 by
SAIL BOOKS
34 Commercial Wharf
Boston, Massachusetts 02110

Foreword

Ask any non-sailor about sails and you are likely to get a description of 'those beautifully colored, balloon sails' – spinnakers. Although they may not know the proper name, anyone who has seen a spinnaker remembers the color, the size, and the excitement that is displayed by this family of downwind sails. Even veteran racing and cruising sailors acknowledge a certain magic associated with spinnakers. Some revere a spinnaker's ability to move a boat in the lightest of winds; others fear a spinnaker's size and the power it can generate. Perhaps this fear stems from a lack of understanding of spinnakers in general – how they are designed, how they are built, and how they are properly flown.

In this book R R King (known as Bunty by all his sailing friends) provides all that is necessary to allay those fears. *Spinnaker* will be a valuable source of information for all sailors, from racers to cruisers, beginners to experts.

At first thought one might ask 'can enough be written on spinnakers to fill a book?' After reading what Bunty has written the experienced sailor will realize how much he has forgotten, and the novice will learn all the tricks of how to use a spinnaker to race or cruise downwind with more speed, excitement, and control.

Bunty explains the evolution of spinnakers, as it has taken place over approximately the last hundred years. Starting with the manufacture of the specialized cloths used, he discusses the various design elements that are critical in building downwind sails. Bunty's description of the various types of spinnakers from the basic, all purpose sail to the most specialized cuts, provides a valuable overview of the many different types of spinnaker that have evolved for both racing and cruising.

The equipment used to fly a spinnaker is often viewed as a confusing mass of oddly named gear. Foreguys, reaching struts, topping lifts – they are all clearly described and their usage explained. A quick glance of the table of contents will quickly convince the reader that Bunty has covered just about everything that not only should happen, but everything that can happen when flying a spinnaker. His tips on how to properly trim and handle spinnakers are particularly valuable and should give sailors skill and confidence in all types of conditions. This is the sort of information that every crew member should know and understand.

I can envision *Spinnaker* being used for years as a reference book for downwind sailing. *Spinnaker* is a book that every sailor should include in his library.

Frederick E 'Ted' Hood   *iii*

Contents

Acknowledgement

For this book to exist at all, I have to acknowledge the part played by Messrs Hood Sailmakers. During the years I worked for Ted Hood, running the loft at Lymington in England, I had the unique opportunity of co-operating with him and those other two innovators Chris Bouzaid and Robby Doyle, not only concerning spinnakers but also over all aspects of the sailmaker's art. Without this experience I could not have covered the subject to the extent I have done. I am grateful to Ted Hood for his kind foreword, and for permission to use some of the photographs in this book.

My son David and Proctor Metal Masts were kind enough to help me prepare sketches for Mike Collins' beautiful drawings; Samuel Courtauld Ltd and ICI Fibres were most helpful regarding sailcloth; the Offshore Racing Council's rule book was constantly by my side, and Keith Ludlow of the RORC Rating Office kindly checked some of my measurement explanations (but any faults remaining are mine, not his).

Finally I have to acknowledge the help that was given me by Jeremy Howard-Williams. Had he not stood over me constantly urging me to produce manuscript, drawings and all the other items that go to make up a book of this sort and then finally knocking it into shape for me, there is absolutely no doubt that it would have never been published.

Introduction

Sailing started down wind, when man first realised that a bush or other bulky cargo in a boat would help his progress in that direction. The ancient Egyptians found that the prevailing wind helped them to travel up the Nile, so that they could then come back on the current. Dugout canoes could be propelled by holding up animal skins. The Norsemen stretched sewn sails on yards to run before the winds funneling down their fjords. But the art of persuading a boat to go the other way, into the wind, took a long time to develop; it is little wonder that the square riggers, with their vast areas of canvas, grew in popularity. It is also little wonder that they were so bulky; their towering topsides were, if anything, a help down wind and they certainly added to accommodation and to visibility from their lofty decks.

Outside Europe vessels were less top heavy from an earlier time. Man was beginning to realise that he could travel other than dead before the wind, as the Polynesians moved among their islands in the prevailing beam winds, and the lateen rig evolved in the eastern Mediterranean. But as the windward going vessel became more efficient, its down wind ability diminished. Just as the gaff rig superseded the square sail in Europe, so the bermudan mainsail ousted the gaff, with a resulting loss of area when running. Large jibs were boomed out opposite the mainsail, until inevitably a sail was developed specially for the purpose when racing.

The spinnaker had been born.

The date can be pinpointed with a certain amount of accuracy. On 5th June 1865 a certain Mr William Gordon unveiled the jib he had specially cut in his own sail loft at Southampton, England, set it flying from his boat *Niobe*'s topmast and boomed it out opposite to his mainsail during a race in the Solent. It did him so well in the match races which were popular at the time that he sold one like it to the owner of a boat called *Sphinx*. We are left with several choices as to how the name of the sail evolved. There are those who say that it is a corruption of the word 'sphinxer', from

1

the second boat's name, and there are those who prefer Tom Diaper's version. Writing in his memoirs in 1939 (*Tom Diaper's Log*, published in 1950), he relates that his grandfather had been the professional skipper of the *Niobe* when she first set the sail nearly a hundred years earlier, and his family tradition had it that, when the new sail was first set, one of the deck hands had admired it.

'Now that is the sail to make her spin.'

From this remark is supposed to have come 'spin-maker' and thus 'spinaker' or 'spinnaker'. Whether you go along with this, or the derivation from the name *Sphinx*, or even (as some do) with an association with the spinning properties given to a ship's steering by the small triangular sail set under the bowsprit to counter weather helm (and sometimes known as a 'Jimmy Green'), what is on record is that the word 'spinniker' appeared in *The Field* on 18th August 1866. Editor of that redoubtable British sporting periodical at the time was Mr Dixon Kemp, renowned for his *Manual of Yachting and Boat Sailing*; the word appeared as 'spinnaker' later the same year in the *Yachting Magazine*.

For over fifty years the sail remained cut rather like a full light genoa, with luff and leech quite distinct and of different lengths. Its change to symmetry came in the late 1920's, when one or two owners started having spinnakers made with equal sides to help in the gybe; one of these was Sven Salen who used such a sail on his 6-metre *Maybe* from Ratsey & Lapthorn's New York loft in 1927. The sails were made in two halves, joined together with a seam down the middle, so that they could be set either way round. It was not long before they were being set round the outside of the forestay rather than inside it.

The luff and leech of these sails were straight, and shaping was almost exclusively introduced by means of adding a curve to the central seam. The result was a highly inefficient deep bellied sail with pronounced curl at the edges, which could only be set with any reasonable hope of success while the wind was well aft. This did not particularly concern owners at the time, because the genoa jib was evolving to give added area with the wind abeam, so there was little pressure to increase the scope of the spinnaker. But the time was to come.

The spinnaker as it has emerged today is a highly developed sail, which requires skill if the best is to be got from it. This skill is no hidden art which only a few exceptional people are capable of acquiring. It is something which may be mastered by anybody given time, patience and above all practice. The saying that practice makes perfect is very true in the case of spinnaker handling, for you will only become good at it if you do it over and over again. In doing this you will evolve your own techniques, and I hope in this book to have laid out the procedures in such a manner that you will have a good basis on which to work.

Many people develop a kind of love-hate relationship with the spinnaker, and it has often been said that this sail is the easiest to hoist but requires the most courage. This, however, is a misconception because, while it does require a degree of knowledge to set properly, it will behave itself if handled correctly. If sail handling and trimming is first practised in light weather, the crew will soon master the basic procedures which are essential if the sail is to be easily controlled in stronger winds.

Sailing down wind in light airs with just a mainsail and jib can be a tedious business, which a spinnaker can turn into a pleasant experience. Not only does it add interest to crew drill, but the extra speed is in itself a powerful stimulant to morale. So the cruising man can not only get to his destination more quickly, but he can enjoy himself more while doing so.

It is worth mentioning here that there appears to have been some departure from tradition in the naming of the parts of the sail. Should the edges be luffs or leeches? I am sure that in the days of the square rigger they would have been referred to as leeches, in which case the term clew for the corner between leech and foot would be correct. However, in talking about the sail when it is lying inert, we refer to its edges as luffs, but still call the corners clews. It appears, therefore, that tradition has been broken, but I would suggest that we stay with the usage of this century and call them luffs and clews as generic terms. The spinnaker has been around long enough to build a tradition in its own right. However, when the sail is set, it is sensible and less confusing to talk about the tack as being that corner which is held out by the pole, and the luff as the edge which runs from there to the head; the other side has the clew and the leech. Being symmetrical, these names change as the sail is gybed from one side to the other.

There are, of course, other ways of going down wind, and I shall cover these to the extent of giving mention to twin running sails and the square sail. And we mustn't forget the whole range of sails which can be set with the spinnaker: staysails of various kinds, slot sails, bloopers and the like.

I hope that this book will help the reader to a better understanding of the spinnaker, so that he will quickly master the art of handling it and get the exhilarating results which such mastery will bring.

1

The Spinnaker Explained

We saw in the Introduction that the spinnaker has been developed in order to give back to the sailing vessel some of the down wind efficiency it lost with the passing of the square rig. To do this it must convert as much wind power into boat speed as possible, within certain limitations.

What are those limitations? First, the sail must be efficient, not only with the wind aft but also when it moves towards and even forward of the beam. Secondly, there must be rules within which racing yachts have to keep, or comparison of boat with boat would be impossible. Thirdly, the sail must be seamanlike in that it shall be controllable under conditions reasonable for its use. Finally, the sailmaker must be able to produce the shape dictated by the limitations just outlined. Let us examine these four criteria in broad terms before getting down to detail later.

Efficiency

To assess efficiency, we need to know something of what happens to the wind as it passes over the sails of a yacht. Apart from when it is blowing from a sector about fifteen degrees either side of dead astern, the wind passes over a spinnaker from luff to leech in much the same way as it covers a jib. The spinnaker, therefore, can be considered as an extra large headsail with certain advantages and disadvantages.

Advantages. A spinnaker has a good deal more area than a jib, so that it can convert more wind power into thrust. It also has an adjustable tack, which can be shifted through a large arc in order to promote efficient trim. The sail is usually made from light material, which responds readily to soft breezes and the relatively lighter apparent wind speeds encountered when running.

Disadvantages. The luff is never straight as it is with a jib, so that the spinnaker's up wind performance suffers; similarly, the belly is so pronounced, even in so-called flat cut spinnakers, that once again its performance up wind reduces to the point where it will not set at all; this occurs before the boat comes hard on the wind. Even where a spinnaker can be persuaded to set with an apparent wind some 50–60 degrees off the bow, the belly in the leech is often sufficient to nullify any advantage gained by the extra area, and it brakes the boat through excessive heel and, indeed, a rear component to the thrust; light nylon stretches quite a lot and aggravates this problem.

The spinnaker, therefore, must convert wind power into thrust much as the headsail does. To achieve this it must deflect the direction of the wind, setting up a system of lift and drag into which we need not go too deeply here. Suffice it to say that the luff should ensure a free entry for the wind, and that the leech area should not be so bellied as to cause the escaping air to turn too much to windward, and thus into the lee side of the mainsail. To achieve maximum efficiency, the sail should normally be spread as far away from the mainsail as possible so as to trap more air. Figure 1 shows different trim combinations, with varying apparent wind directions, as compared with a standard size genoa.

Rules

Although this free-flying sail appears to be without limit in size, this cannot be the case where racing boats are concerned. The first spinnakers to appear may well have been unmeasured, but this utopian state of affairs did not last long and the legislators began to impose limits.

In the first instance our ancestral rule makers found it relatively easy to limit size by stating how far apart the three corners should be. They, or perhaps their sons, were quick to spot the ways in which cunning sailmakers were putting more and more cloth into the sail by devious tricks of the trade. So cunning were these masters of the cloth that, in about the span of two generations, the spinnaker evolved from something that looked more akin to a rather full genoa, into the much larger and more scientifically designed parachute spinnaker which immediately preceded the sail we know today.

These generations of rule makers obviously could not allow this to continue unchecked, so all sorts of restrictions were evolved, and even today arguments as to what is best still linger. Matters are not helped by the fact that the spinnaker is one of the most difficult of sails to measure accurately.

If extravagant sails, which will not only be impossible to handicap but will also be unseamanlike, are not to emerge, therefore, it is obvious that there must be workable regulations within which spinnakers must be controlled. There are three basic rules under which the sail may normally   5

Spinnaker

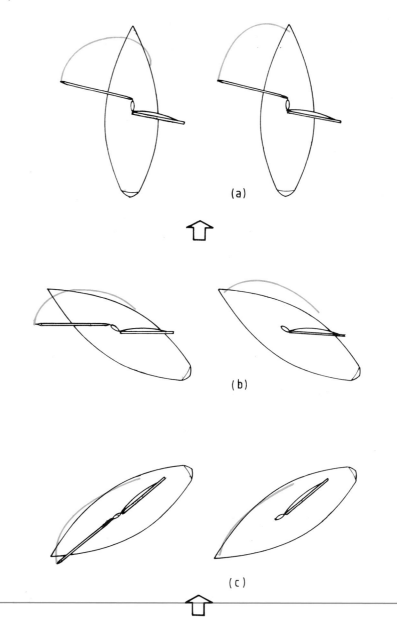

1. *Spinnaker Trim 1.* Spinnaker and genoa are compared on a run (a), and broad reach (b) and a close reach (c). See also Fig 27 on page 125 to compare with (c) as to whether the spinnaker is acting efficiently.

be allowed; in order of restriction they are:
1. One-design.
2. Restricted.
3. Free.

One-Design. As the name implies, a one-design sail should be the same in all respects as every other sail made to the same rule. In practice there are few classes where the one-design concept is complete, because weight and colour of cloth may usually be varied. The old International One-Design class (a boat developed in the mid thirties, based on the International 6-metre) enforced a standard cloth, even to the pale blue colour, but classes such as the Daring (a boat based on the International 5·5-metre) and the Dragon allow variation in colour and cloth weight but not in shape. In some cases a rule will permit spinnakers smaller than the maximum sail. Uniformity which needs to be ensured is achieved either by including detailed sail measurements in the rules, together with limitations on the amount of shaping which the sailmaker may introduce, or else by nominating class sailmakers who are required to stick to an approved pattern. The Dragon is an example of the former and the IOD of the latter.

Restricted. This is the classification which embraces most of the spinnakers produced all over the world. Restrictions may take the form of limiting the length of the luffs and the cross measurement at any point (either one maximum measurement throughout the height of the sail, or else a maximum foot measurement together with a wider permitted cross measurement at half height). We shall see later how the complex curves of the three dimensional shape of a spinnaker make its precise measurement one of the more difficult tasks of the rule maker. The IOR is a good example of this type of sail, and there are many dinghy classes which come into the same category if they are not one-design. There are also some classes which limit the overall perimeter of the sail (total length of both luffs plus foot), but allow freedom of shape within that restriction.

Free. This rule either has no restrictions whatsoever, other than those imposed by common sense and a respect for the elements, or else it limits one or two controlling factors such as spinnaker pole length and/or the foot of the sail. This effectively controls the rest of the sail within certain maxima, because there is also the natural limit on the luffs imposed by the height of the halyard sheave above deck—itself almost always controlled. The international metre classes rated under the IYRU rule (12-metres, 6-metres etc) usually limit the foot but allow complete freedom elsewhere. This, of course, results in sails of all shapes and sizes, but a pattern eventually emerges outside of which it is seldom profitable to stray.

Control

It is no good having a spinnaker which responds to all or any of the foregoing requirements, if the crew cannot set it easily and then control it properly. It must be possible to hoist it in all suitable winds, trim it to best effect, and gybe it from side to side. Sheer size may trap more air, but it makes for difficulty in control, and the 12-metres are an example of this: their light weather spinnakers are usually more efficient if they are fairly limited in size, particularly in the head, as against those which try to cram maximum area into the sail in an effort to trap more wind; in very light airs, the extra weight of cloth alone is often enough to collapse a maxi-sail, while the smaller rival continues to set.

Hoisting. Hoisting a spinnaker requires certain gear which we shall examine later. Basically the sail must be stowed in a convenient container so that it behaves predictably as it comes out. In practice this usually involves some kind of special bag or turtle, into which the sail is packed so that the head and clews are protruding; halyard, sheet and guy can then be snapped on at the location of hoisting. If the luffs have been carefully flaked so that they have no twists in them, the sail will emerge from its turtle by the head without any tangles when the halyard is hoisted. This desirable state of affairs can be helped if the luffs are pulled out straight before bagging, and bands of rotten cotton or rubber are placed round the sail to prevent ravelling; this is called 'stopping' and is more fully described in Chapter 6. A particular advantage of stopping is that large sails do not deploy in strong winds, before they are fully hoisted and then broken out deliberately when all is ready.

Trim. The two principal objects of good spinnaker trim are, first, to get the sail as far away from the mainsail and into undisturbed air as possible and, secondly, so to arrange the spinnaker that wind power is converted into forward thrust rather than sideways pressure. It stands to reason that it is no good trapping a lot of unused air if you are only going to use it to heel the boat or even drag it backwards. To achieve these two objects, the spinnaker tack can be moved around the foredeck on the end of its pole, in that it may be shifted outboard, and its height may be moved up and down; in addition the sheet may, of course, be played like that of any other sail. With this amount of control, the sail can easily be set in the wrong manner, and a study of its problems will be repaid. The converse is also true, that it is often possible to improve the set of a spinnaker in almost all conditions if the theory is understood. Study it therefore.

The Gybe. When a boat gybes under spinnaker, the transfer of the mainsail from one side to the other is quick and easy. Due to the complexity of the equipment involved, however, the spinnaker cannot simply swing across the boat in the same way (apart from anything else, any sail which automatically switches sides when tacking or gybing presents its opposite surface to the wind on the new board; the spinnaker cannot turn inside out when it is set and remain under control). So there has to be a drill for partly dismantling the gear used to establish and trim the sail, moving it all to the other side of the boat, and then setting it all up again. This is the gybe, and its object is always the same: to transfer the spinnaker to the other side of the boat exactly when needed, without collapsing the sail in the process and thus losing drive. There are many and varied systems, depending on size of boat and sail, and also on the owner's personal preference.

Thus we shall be considering a sail unique in the boat's wardrobe. When set it does not have any of its edges restrained by a spar or stay, and both its tack and clew may be moved about at will. It is certainly the largest sail in the boat, which in itself surely endears it to many. The very freedom of the sail ensures that the manner in which it is set requires a certain expertise, and this is where the element of challenge comes in. Such is the fascination of the spinnaker that rarely does one go for a sail without hearing requests from the crew to 'up chute'.

Although the sail is greater in area than any other, when running it can be set in much more true wind than the genoa, less than half its area, will tolerate when going to windward. This is easy to explain, for it is a matter of relative apparent wind speeds. Let us take the following example. If the true wind is 12 knots, when you are going to windward at 5 knots the apparent wind will be in the order of 17 knots (the true speed plus the speed you are moving towards it), which is certainly not light genoa weather; indeed, smaller boats may well be using a smaller headsail, if they are not reefed. On turning round and going the other way with a following breeze, the boat with a spinnaker flying will be moving at perhaps 6 knots. As you are now moving away from the true wind, its apparent speed is diminished by your boat's speed, which drops it to 6 knots – almost floater weather. This is why such a large sail relative to the sailplan can be carried.

We see then that the apparent wind speed is reduced when running so that we may spread before it a large area of sail. Because we are not prepared to tolerate a yard at the masthead, we have to hoist our sail to a single point, and have devised the largest sail the rule makers have seen fit to let us have, in such a way that the wind will hold it in shape.

Why then does the sail become so much more difficult to use as the wind comes round onto the beam or to a close reach? There are two separate reasons for this. The first is the apparent wind speed problem. As soon as the boat is turned off a run, through a reach and up onto the wind, the wind speed across the deck increases rapidly until what was proving to be a light run will turn into a fast broad reach, a lively beam reach, and very probably a hectic close reach.

The second reason is that as soon as the wind is on the beam the sail will usually be too full, and to get the best boat speed a flatter reaching spinnaker is needed for aerodynamic efficiency. As the boat is sailed still closer to the wind, even this sail will be too full and will collapse. The closer to the wind a sail is carried the flatter it must be cut.

When it comes to a question of a race, the spinnaker contributes a great deal to the success of the boat. The crew who are able to obtain the best performance from their sails by careful trimming will gain. The spinnaker has long been an essential part of a racing boat's kit; the argument may be extended, because one spinnaker is insufficient for a boat which wants to be competitive, and a wardrobe of sails is necessary if the full range of conditions is to be catered for.

Gear. It is not possible to consider the spinnaker in isolation, and the gear necessary to hoist and control the sail must be scrutinised as carefully as the sail itself. The ability to work to fine degrees of trim requires gear that is well developed and capable of doing the job efficiently. Just as there are many sailmakers who can produce a good spinnaker, so there are many spar and fitting makers who are capable of producing the right gear. While there are basic rules for the layout of this equipment, there are many variations within those rules, so considerable thought should be given to this aspect. Hoisting and trim do not in themselves involve complex equipment beyond blocks and winches, but the gybe is another matter. We shall examine later some of these drills, so suffice it to say here that robust and efficient gear is essential to all of them. If you are going in for a spinnaker and all which that entails, therefore, be prepared for some considerable expense.

Sailmaking—Cloth

We have seen that spinnakers have always been made of light material because, when a boat is running, the apparent wind is always less than the true wind. In the early days, light cotton was used but, apart from one or two experiments with rayon, silk, and polyester, nylon has proved to be the universal cloth since World War II.

Nylon is the generic name used to indicate any of a group of plastic materials which were developed in the 1930's as a derivative of carbon. Invented by research teams working in New York and London (hence its name), under Wallace Carothers of Harvard University and the duPont company of the USA, nylon was used extensively during World War II for parachutes but it was not until after that time that it was used for sails.

For sailcloth, nylon is spun off into a filament from the liquid state, and it is then cold drawn to some 400 times its existing length. This makes the yarn very thin, aligns the molecules and increases tenacity by as much as five times. The basic properties of the material are good for spinnakers. It has good elasticity and recovery before breaking, its wet strength is 80–90 per cent of its dry strength, and its breaking strain only falls by about 15 per cent when it is knotted or hitched. Its low specific gravity of 1·14 makes it highly suitable for light weight fabrics, because its fibre diameter is large for its weight, thus enabling a good cover factor to be achieved when weaving.

Melting point is a trifle low by textile standards, being about 250°C in air; an iron of 180°C will cause the material to stick or the individual threads to fuse, while 230°C causes serious damage. Therefore a spinnaker should never be ironed (nylon is light enough for the creases to blow themselves out as the sail 'drip-dries') and, if overheated, the material turns yellow but at this stage the damage has already been done.

Chemically stable, nylon is resistant to many of the chemicals which it is likely to meet when used as sailcloth. In particular, solvents used in dry cleaning liquids are normally safe enough, although acids such as formic and phenol (carbolic) will dissolve it, so care is always advised.

Although mildew can form on dirt particles trapped in the weave, the material itself is not affected, but it is subject to weakening through prolonged exposure to sunlight or certain pollutant atmospheres. If burned, it melts and drops away in globules, but the general fire risk is low.

Synthetic yarns are graded according to two standards. The first of these is *denier*, known to women the world over as a measure of fineness in stockings or tights, and is derived from the silk industry. In particular, it is the weight in grams of 9,000 metres of the yarn concerned: a cop of yarn containing 9,000 metres which weighed a total of 100 grams would be described as 100 denier yarn. If two or more yarns are twisted together into a single thread, the denier of the final product is the sum of those from which it was composed.

The system which has recently been replacing the denier is based on the *tex*. This is a unit of measurement which weighs 1,000 metres of yarn, instead of 9,000 metres as with the denier. The tex can be divided as in the metric system into millitex, decitex (often written d'tex) and tex, and it will be seen that 1 tex = 10 decitex = 1,000 militex = 9 denier.

Weaving of spinnaker nylon is straightforward, and the cloth is usually constructed relatively square, that is to say that threads on warp and weft or fill are of equal or nearly equal decitex. Often a doubled thread is regularly introduced into both warp and weft, at perhaps quarter inch or half centimetre intervals, in order to reinforce the weave in what is known as a rip-stop pattern. The resulting material is then subjected to finishing processes like most other synthetic sailcloths, including scouring, cleaning, heat shrinking and setting, and calendering; it may also have resin fillers added to improve stability and impermeability. A soft finish with a flexible handle is usually good, though care should be taken that this has not been achieved through use of resin fillers which can delaminate. Largely a thing of the past, some cheap cloths may still show marble crazing and a marked deterioration in the 'blow' test (breathing through the cloth) after a sample has been crushed in the hand. A stiff finish ensures a stable cloth, but sometimes at the expense of tear strength. Start a tear with a pair of scissors and then pull apart by hand. Both types of cloth will give, but the stiff one will usually go more readily than the soft one.

As is well known, nylon takes dyes better in sailmaking weights than Terylene or Dacron, thus allowing colourful patterns. Given certain combinations of moisture and heat, the dyes may run. Thus, a damp multi-coloured spinnaker stuffed into a bag in the forepeak can result in the dyes of the darker reds and blues running into the lighter yellows and whites. Once this has happened, there is no cure.

Because thread deniers are somewhat standardised in the commercial market, sailcloth nylon has settled down to roughly the following weights, depending on the individual weave and finishing process.

oz/yd × 28½″ USA standard	oz/yd² UK standard	gm/m² metric
0·5	0·65	22
0·8	1·0	34
1·2	1·5	51
1·5	1·9	65
2·2	2·75	93
2·6	3·3	112

Nylon thus has many good qualities as spinnaker material. In desirable relationship, it is lightweight, pliable, crease-resistant, and can be woven to a high cover factor, which makes it relatively non-porous; in addition it can be dyed easily, thus making it aesthetically pleasing. Finally, spinnakers need a certain amount of elasticity to help them take up their buxom shape before the wind. Nylon has a degree of inherent stretch which is accentuated by the very lightness of the cloth weights employed –usually in the range between ½ and 2 ounces (20–70gm/m^2).

In common with any woven material, nylon distorts or stretches more readily on the bias than on the warp and weft or fill. Pull it along or across the run of the panels, therefore, and distortion is low but, as soon as the load comes off the threadline, it will stretch out of shape. This has to be borne in mind by the sailmaker when he decides how to cut a particular sail, and explains some of the exotic patterns sometimes seen as designers try to eliminate unwanted stretch in the complex curves of specialised spinnakers.

Mylar is a super-thin super-strong synthetic film ('it's so thin, it's only got one side' say the makers), which is used in composite construction of sailcloth. For spinnakers, the cloth is transparent and has Kevlar threads bonded in every quarter inch or so, reminiscent of the familiar rip-stop pattern. The sail is shaped by bonding rather than sewing the various seams, and tears are effectively stopped by the Kevlar which won't break but which merely bunches up on itself. As with most innovations, the cost is high during the development stage, but as it leaves the realm of the ultra-racing machine and becomes standard equipment not only for round the buoy racing but for cruising as well, so the price comes down. The advantage is a weightsaving of over fifty per cent.

Sailmaking—Cuts

As I have said, the first spinnakers were virtually specialised jibs hoisted flying from the masthead and boomed out opposite the mainsail down wind. They were thus traditionally lop-sided sails, with the luff longer than the leech, and were often made with panels running parallel to the leech. This was because the luff still had a heavy wire running along it, which served to prevent undue stretch of the cloth as it met that edge on the bias; the free edge of the leech distorted relatively little because the warp ran all along its straight edge, so that the load was on the threadline.

Symmetrical. When symmetrical sails were introduced in the 1920's, the twin luffs remained substantially straight, largely so that the threadline could remain parallel; this necessitated a seam down the middle of the sail as shown in Fig 2. It was a short step from here to the greater area conferred by rounding the shoulders of the sail, and Herbulot of France developed the inverted chevron with some success just after World War II. Although the panels met the unsupported luffs on the bias, it was found that stretch at the luffs was controllable within reasonable limits. This was achieved through three factors: the improved stability of nylon over light cotton, tightening the seams at the luffs, and use of reinforcing tapes and light wires.

Cross-Cut. In 1951 Ted Hood took this development to its logical conclusion by laying the cloths so that the weft or fill was parallel to the luff at each side. This resulted in some bias at the seam down the middle of the sail, but there were plenty of seams in just the right places so this was controllable by tapering the panels appropriately. The CCA and RORC rules of the time restricted the maximum width of all spinnakers to   *13*

Spinnaker

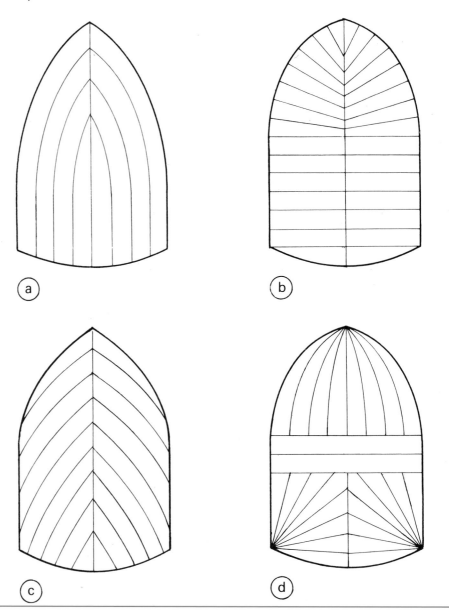

2. *Sail Cuts 1.* (a) Early vertical cut, with seams parallel to the luffs; the shoulders are narrow. (b) Cross cut as developed by Ted Hood, with seams at right angles to the luffs. (c) Chevron cut popularised by Herbulot, with panels arranged to minimise cloth bias at the centre seam. (d) Modern tri-radial developed from the Banks star-cut. Note that the radial panels are narrower than the horizontal ones.

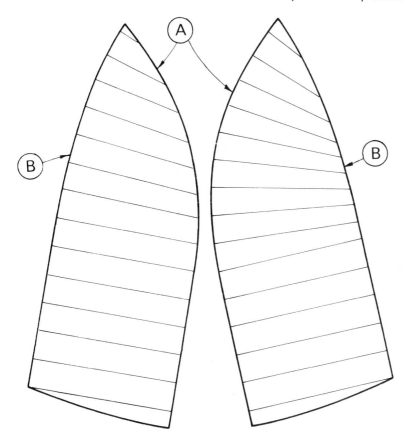

3. *Sail Cuts 2.* Two spinnakers folded in half down their centre seams A. The left hand sail has cloths running at right angles from the luffs B; the sail is made in two halves and sewn together down the centre seam A. The cloths in the right hand sail are laid so that they cross the centrefold at right angles; the spinnaker may thus be made in one piece with no centre seam, although one may be found in some sails to simplify production.

the same all the way up the sail (as does the IOR rule today); this produced a rectangular shape in the lower half of the sail, which encouraged a horizontal cut because the panels remained at right angles to both luffs and centre seam for this part of the sail. Threadlines thus ran parallel to the foot (along the warp) and luffs (along the weft or fill) and the centre seam in the lower half (along the weft), thereby avoiding too much distortion. It will be noted that the cloths at the head were laid to run away from the luffs at right angles, so that bias angle was confined to the centre seam in the upper half of the sail.

Spherical. But Hard Sails thought why stop there? If the Herbulot chevron cut did not cause too much trouble at the luffs with its cloths on the bias, surely the centre seam could be eliminated altogether? To understand this properly, we have to look briefly at how a spinnaker is cut out and, indeed, measured. The only way in which the convex curve can   *15* be made to lie even nearly flat on the loft floor is if it is folded in half down the middle, so that the two clews lie on top of each other and half the sail is presented in profile. It will be seen from the representation of a typical sail at Fig 2 that its head cloths can either be laid so that they run away from the luffs at right angles, thus presenting bias angles at the centre-fold so that they have to be cut and sewn at this point; or else they can run at right angles away from the centrefold so that they do not need to be cut and sewn, but in which case they present a large bias angle to the luffs. Hard Sails developed this seamless cut particularly for those sails made to the free rule, where there was no restriction on the width at half height other than what could be made to set properly. It produced a well setting sail of considerable area, which was rather like part of a sphere, and they christened it the spherical cut. Other names, such as the orbital cut, have since been given to it by other sailmakers.

Reaching Sails

Owners had been quick to appreciate that the spinnaker was not only a race-winner down wind, but that its area should be made to pay dividends whenever it could be brought efficiently to bear. For a long while, however, the euphoria brought on by the arrival of the genoa, coupled with the deep belly of the spinnakers of the period, meant that a beam reach was just about as close to the wind as most boats tried to carry the larger sail for a long time. If they wanted to make a spinnaker which would work well on a reach, sailmakers devoted their energies to narrowing and flattening the head by means of shortening the head panels and tapering various seams as presented by the cross or horizontal cut. When folded in half down the middle and looked at on the floor, the curve taken up by the centrefold near the head will indicate the depth of belly, while the line of the luffs will reveal the breadth of the shoulders: too little and the sail will be a narrow gutted affair, suitable perhaps for stiffish winds; too much and the shoulders will collapse unless the wind is dead aft.

As well as being flatter with smaller shoulders than a regular spinnaker, a reaching spinnaker may also be smaller in overall dimensions. Unless the boat is of relatively heavy displacement, or for some other reason is particularly able to carry a spinnaker set shy, the width of the sail might be as much as 15 per cent less than the maximum, and up to 5 per cent shorter than the maximum on the luffs. The exact amount will be decided by the sailmaker and must be considered along with the design of the hull and sailplan. At first many owners jibbed at the loss of area, but they were soon converted to the idea when the realised that, in this instance, shape is more important than area. Today reaching spinnakers are usually either tri-radial or star-cut sails (see below).

On boats of 35ft LOA and over, the gap between this sail and the runner is often found to be too large, or perhaps the runner is too light to

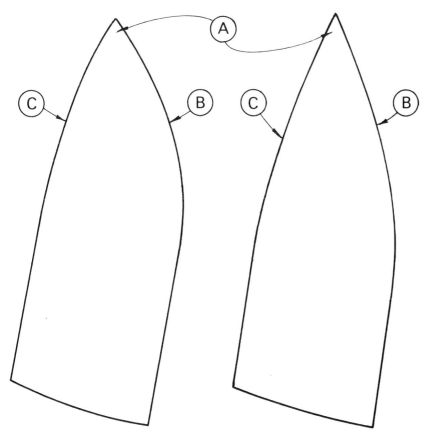

4.   *Sail Cuts 3.*   Comparing two spinnakers, both folded in half luff upon luff down the centre seam. The left hand one is the fuller running sail, while that on the right is a flatter reaching sail – note its narrower head angle A, flatter centre seam B and smaller shoulders C.

use in stronger winds when the boat can still carry a large sail. In this case the suitability of the reaching spinnaker depends on the type of sailing to be done. A sail made from heavier cloth, say $1\frac{1}{2}$oz, up to full width and luff length but with reduced shoulders and cut flatter than the light runner, reaches well and is a useful sail to set in round the cans racing, when course changes are many.

Radial Head. By now sailmakers were giving a good deal of thought to the stresses in the spinnaker. Various combinations of the different patterns appeared, as first one and then another was tried in attempts to control the shape more rigidly. The radial head emerged as a solution to the problem at the upper part of the sail, on the grounds that the local stresses naturally radiated from the head. This was later coupled with a multitude of different cuts, so that sails resembling patchwork quilts appeared from various lofts.

Star-Cut. The fact that the spinnaker has no mast or stay to support any of the loadings in the sail, which is only supported at the head and clews, finally persuaded the theorists that all the stresses must radiate from the three corners. The radial head had proved itself to be sufficiently efficient to warrant trying the method on the clews as well, and it was Bruce Banks Sails who took the matter to its proper conclusion and evolved the star-cut, where all the panels meet at the middle of the sail from radial cut corners. At last the problem of too much bias stretch at the centre was licked, and spinnakers with plenty of area which did not develop too much belly could be produced for reaching purposes. Strangely enough, it was not until later that the tri-radial was developed, which has the same corners as the star-cut, but includes a number of cross panels in the middle to introduce the fullness required.

The configuration is not confined to reaching sails and Bruce Banks does make a general purpose full sized star-cut. However, the cut is much more expensive than the somewhat simpler tri-radial and I doubt whether it is that much more effective for running conditions. That it produces a good stable sail is without question, but one can over-engineer.

The star-cut is rightly popular, but the modern boat with its light displacement and low wetted area cannot take full advantage of it except in a narrow performance range. Under the IOR sail limitations it has become less necessary to have too specialised a close winded sail; as soon as the boat is sailed further off the wind a larger and fuller area can be carried, so a more versatile sail is called for. This emerged as the tri-radial, or shooting star as Ratsey & Lapthorn called their version when they introduced it, and is essentially a star-cut sail with several horizontal panels through the middle to allow fullness to develop.

The star-cut is probably the most publicised and talked about type of spinnaker, and is a familiar sight on the water with its three pointed star pattern – itself a measure of the sail's success. Bruce Banks can take full credit for its innovation and development. The sail first became prominent on *Longbow* during the Admiral's Cup in 1969, although he had used the cut on some of the 12-metre spinnakers he had made for *Sovereign* in 1963/4. In the early days he made the sails in plain colour, and the story goes that *Longbow's* owner David Macauley, who was in

1. *Opposite* This radial head spinnaker is being carried rather too close to the wind; divide it down the middle and note how the rear half is pulling aft and countering the thrust from the forward half. Lowering the pole would straighten the luff and pull the sail forward. This would enable the sheet to be eased and the leech freed, correcting the tendency for the wind to be turned into the back of the mainsail. The airflow could then escape easily thus reducing drag.
Hood Sailmakers

2. *Above* A beautiful example of a star-cut (made, incidentally, by the inventor) on *Impulse* of South Africa.

Bruce Banks Sails

3. *Right* This enormous tri-radial is being set on an 18ft Sydney Harbour Skiff. The patch in the middle reinforces the attachment point of a retrieval line. It would appear that the problems of handling the large area in such a small boat have already caused a tear at some time.

Dawn Hughes

4. *Opposite Carpetbagger*
is setting a small flat super
star-cut on a very close
reach, with a high clewed
reacher under it, set from a
reefed tack position. Note
that the boat to windward is
using a double-head rig (and
pointing higher).
Hood Sailmakers

advertising, had Banks take out the central star and replace it with cloth of a contrasting colour, thus launching the pattern on the sailing scene.

The construction is a stable one, as the cloth does not distort too much under the heavy loads which can be experienced when sailing close to the wind. In addition, the three radial corners pulling on the centre of the sail tend to flatten it. This of course is a desirable thing for a reaching spinnaker; if it were to grow fuller, it would not be so good.

The star-cut is usually made from a heavier cloth than a regular running sail, with strongly made reinforcements at the corners. This makes it also suitable as a heavy weather running sail, so that it serves a dual role. When used in storm conditions, it must be remembered that the sail is made flat and therefore must be set with the pole low.

The main danger is that it is possible to set it *too* close to the wind. The sail can be kept full even though it is strapped in so hard that it makes the boat wallow and develop a lot of leeway – the quickest way to sail sideways out of a race. The mainsail has to be over-sheeted, which adds to the trouble and is itself an indicator that you have problems. Under these conditions mentally divide the spinnaker down the middle, and assess whether the rear half is pulling you backwards. If it is, then you would probably be better off with a genoa or a double headsail rig.

It can be seen that, although the starcut is by design a specialised sail which, on first inspection, may not be everyone's choice, especially in a limited inventory, the fact that it can double as a heavy weather sail makes it earn its place in the sail locker, even in a two-spinnaker inventory. Whether in fact a star-cut or a tri-radial reacher is chosen really depends on the size and design of boat.

Super Star-cut.   This is not, as its name might imply, a larger star-cut, but is smaller and flatter than its full size sister; it is made from a heavier (2oz or more) cloth and strongly reinforced. As with the general reaching spinnaker, its dimensions are similarly reduced, which enables it to be carried more effectively, and it has proved on many boats to be a faster sail than the regular star-cut. This is particularly true on light displacement boats which do not demand the extra sail area. Being so strong, the super star-cut is a natural for heavy weather purposes.

Light Weather

In light weather the temptation is to cram on as much sail as possible, with a view to catching what wind there is. This idea is about as outmoded as the square riggers which gave birth to it, and we have already briefly touched on its falseness when it comes to spinnakers – largely because of their requirement to be self-supporting. We shall return to this theme below. Bearing in mind that any boat speed when running will reduce still further the already low velocity of the true wind, the principal requirement of a light weather spinnaker is that it shall set at all under the

very light pressures in the sail. To this end it must above all not weigh too much or it will collapse. This postulates a light cloth and not too much of it; aerodynamic shape comes second to getting the thing to set at all.

The Floater. This sail was named by Hoods many years ago, when a very light cloth was developed which contained yarns made from a synthetic material which had a specific gravity of less than one, thereby allowing it to float in water. Hence the name 'floater', which soon caught on as the name for any spinnaker fabric with a weight of less than half an ounce per yard. The sail was developed for 12-metre racing and was first used on *Intrepid*, giving her the enviable ability to pull out of a hole in the wind, to her obvious advantage. There is no doubt that the gossamer material will fill when a normal spinnaker will be in trouble, and the floater has become a popular sail to be found on the majority of top racing boats. It may be used with up to seven or eight knots of apparent wind.

In shape the floater is much like a running spinnaker, but it has been found advantageous to make it a little flatter, with smaller shoulders and tighter luffs. In keeping with the weight of the cloth, the whole sail is made very light with small corner patches and lighter luff tapes than are used on the equivalent regular sail; the sheet should be similarly lightweight.

Floater Star-cut. This sail, as its name implies, is a close reaching star-cut made from floater material. Its use is limited, for it can only be set in very light airs when close reaching. When sailing offshore, where boat speed is often more important than the precise course, this sail may be set quite close to the wind; as boat speed increases, so does the apparent wind speed. If the wardrobe must be limited, this sail may double up as a normal floater, as there is a school of thought which says that a spinnaker for ghosting should be very flat and have small shoulders, in pursuit of keeping the total weight to the minimum. However, the sail is very expensive to make and perhaps should only be considered by the dedicated racing man where cost is of little consequence.

Heavy Weather

Paradoxically, heavy weather spinnakers and those for very light airs have much the same narrow shape aloft – but for quite different reasons. The light weather sail reduces area in order to cut down weight, so that the sail shall continue to set. The storm spinnaker, on the other hand, needs to avoid too much area as a generality when the boat may very well need to reef, and certainly needs to keep the centre of effort low down in the sailplan.

Storm Spinnaker. A sail for the serious offshore racer, the storm spinnaker is not often found in the sail locker unless heavy winds are part of the local weather pattern. It is the smallest spinnaker that may be successfully carried, being about 8–10 per cent short on the luffs, while the maximum width at the foot will be about 155 per cent instead of the 180 per cent of J for a normal spinnaker; the foot may be cut up in a hollow, both further to reduce area and also to improve visibility forward. A smaller sail would not reach the halyard sheave at the head, nor pass round the forestay to sheet correctly. The sail will be narrower at half height than at the foot and will have hardly any shoulders, and it will of course be made of relatively heavy cloth, probably 2½oz at least; on a big boat, 4oz nylon will almost certainly be used. The reinforcing patches and clew rings will be extra strong.

5. *Overleaf Star-cut v Radial Head.* The difference in shape and pole setting is quite apparent, and it is not surprising that *Noryema* is ahead.

Hood Sailmakers

2

Design
Principles

Now that we have enjoyed a brisk run through the limitations and possibilities of the spinnaker, let us take a closer look at how the sail achieves the shape we require. This will entail a certain amount of repetition, but the subject is sufficiently important to stand it.

Although an exact sail shape can be computed for any point of sailing and any particular wind speed, the result will be at its most efficient only under those specific conditions. In practice, constant conditions are rare and, in any case, it would not be practical to have to change spinnakers every time the wind speed or the boat's heading altered. In addition, the elastic nature of its material means that the sail alters in shape, not only with varying wind strength, but also depending on how it is hoisted and trimmed. The problem is thus to produce a compromise between the optimum calculated shape, and a sail which will be efficient in a wide range of wind speeds and angles. The basic parameters affecting any spinnaker are as follows.

1. *Cloth.* The cloth from which it is made must be resistant to stretch and non-porous.

2. *Wind Gradient.* As you get higher above the water, so the wind gets stronger, so that tall sails encounter more force aloft than short ones.

3. *Compatibility.* The spinnaker must be compatible with other sails likely to be used in conjunction with it—principally the mainsail.

4. *Control.* It must be capable of being controlled by its head and two clews only.

5. *Versatility.* It must work effectively in a reasonable range of weather conditions and wind angles.

6. Shape. As there are no spars or stays to support any edge, the sail must be cut so as to support itself and hold its shape.

All this may lead you to wonder how a spinnaker can ever be made to work to best advantage. Indeed, if you watch any racing fleet, wide differences in performance under spinnaker will be apparent; the faster boats will be getting a better aerodynamic shape from their sails than their slower rivals. So it all comes down to shape, and you will have noticed that the items listed above all lead to this, which I have thus left until last.

Cloth

Like any other sail, the spinnaker turns wind speed into thrust by affecting the airflow. It is no good having a perfectly shaped sail, if the wind is to be allowed to blow straight through a porous material hardly pausing in its passage. Fortunately, modern weaving techniques have made highly porous sailcloth almost a thing of the past, but the sailmaker needs to keep an eye on this problem to see that a rogue supply is not allowed through his screening.

More important is the amount of distortion which a cloth will suffer when loading is put on the bias. Obviously, the heavier the cloth the greater the resistance to stretch if other factors are equal. But the demand is for ever lighter nylon, so the weavers have to struggle continually for more stability in their products.

Wind Gradient

The wind speed within 10–15 feet of the surface of the sea is normally only half what it is at 100 feet. Even above 25 feet the difference is marked, so that spinnakers for dinghies do not normally have the power to lift that those set 30–40 feet up can count on, where the percentage of the speed at 100 feet is up to 80 per cent. Thus the element of lift is more important for shorter sails than those for a taller rig. (See Fig 5,) on page 30.

Compatibility

There is a wide range of sails which are flown with the spinnaker, and they must not get in each other's way. The most important of these other sails is the mainsail, because it is not only nearly always set, but it often affects the windstream before the airflow reaches the spinnaker; it is also large enough to contribute a good proportion of thrust, particularly as its clew can be deployed outside the deckplan so that the sail is spread wide. Backwinding of the mainsail must be avoided whenever possible, so the spinnaker leech needs to be as flat as possible when reaching.

Other subsidiary sails include various staysails and genoas set with their luffs substantially on the boat's centreline, and interference between them and the spinnaker luff must be avoided; this is largely a matter of spinnaker trim rather than shape, but the jib tack must be correctly placed in the fore-triangle.

Finally, the blooper is set when the wind is aft, so that its luff is allowed to sag well to leeward. It is more a matter of cutting the blooper so as not to interfere with the spinnaker rather than vice versa, and more particularly of trimming the subsidiary sail to suit the bigger one rather than the other way round. If the spinnaker has to be set out of trim so that the blooper can be flown to best effect, the result will be poorer performance.

Control

A mainsail has a mast and boom to support and spread its area, and a jib has a stay which supports the luff. Apart from the blooper, the spinnaker is the only sail on board which has all its edges free-floating, so that it must support itself. The blooper, having a fixed tack to contend with as well, is a sail of severely limited application, so that its use is virtually restricted to an apparent wind which is strong enough to deploy it (over seven or eight knots) and blowing from a direction within 30 degrees of dead astern.

The spinnaker, on the other hand, has a movable tack as well as a movable clew, so that it can be adjusted to suit a wide range of wind angles. The sail, however, must still spread and support itself solely through wind action, so it must be cut with this in mind, and this demands that the air shall flow across the sail in an efficient manner.

The equipment to ensure this control is an integral part of the sail, and must be carefully thought out if it is to be efficient in use.

Versatility

Having decided that the spinnaker must be made of good cloth, cut to suit the wind gradient, be compatible with the rest of the wardrobe, and be capable of control without supporting spars or stays, we must not be persuaded to produce a sail of limited application.

The cloth must be light, yet strong and non-porous as we have seen, and the shape must be such that the sail can be used through a wide wind range, otherwise the crew will be for ever changing sails as conditions alter. Thus, a running sail must be capable not only of remaining   *29*

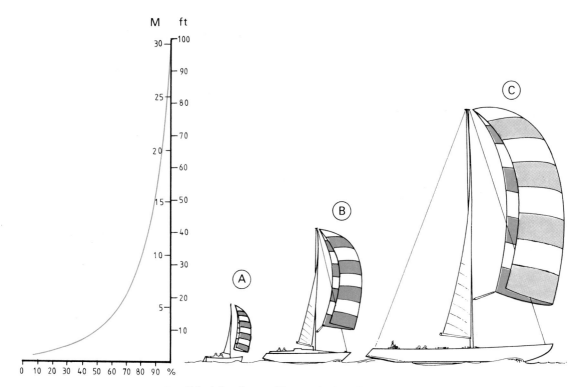

5. *Wind Gradient.* The vertical scale shows feet and metres above sea level, while the horizontal one shows percentage of wind speed at 100 feet or 30 metres. The small dinghy A has little lift compared with the larger yacht B; the maxi-rater C has most lift because the top of her spinnaker is in stronger wind.

aloft when the wind goes towards the beam, but it must still contribute to forward thrust; a special close reaching sail must also be relatively efficient even when the wind frees. There will, of course, be conditions when one type of sail is better than another, so that a boat will need two or three spinnakers if she is to be really competitive. But changing sails can cause loss of time even if it is only through the extra crew weight on the foredeck, so too frequent switching will lose more ground than the more efficient replacement can make up.

Shape

Before we can examine fully the ideal shape of a spinnaker to meet the foregoing requirements, we must decide by what criteria we are going to judge that shape. There are three basic parameters: horizontal section, roach and aspect ratio.

Horizontal Section

We are considering here the shape produced when a section is taken horizontally through the sail and viewed from above. The points which concern us are the depth or flatness of the section, and the severity of the curve at the entry and exit of the wind.

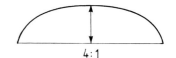

4:1

Flatness. When discussing how flat a spinnaker should be for given conditions, it is convenient to relate the spread of the sail between luffs when set (the chord) to the amount of belly or camber in the sail at that point (depth). Study of hundreds of photographs and a kind of crude photogrammetry, coupled with actual measurement of the sails concerned, has shown that the brief answer to the question of how flat or full an average spinnaker should be, is that it should have a chord to depth ratio of about 5:1. This will vary in practice between 4:1 to give good stability when running, particularly with tall narrow sails, and a high figure of 7:1 for the flatness required in a reaching or for a storm sail. The length of the spinnaker pole and the confines of the sheet fairlead within the beam of the boat will prevent the foot of the sail from being spread wide enough to achieve this deep 4:1 shape, particularly in the lower half, when running or broad reaching but, as the sail opens and lifts, the optimum should be attained from the middle up. When trimming, you should be aiming to get the main body of the sail to take up this sort of horizontal section. When reaching, it is important to be able to move the sheet lead so that the sail can be opened out to achieve a flatter section.

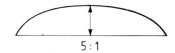

5:1

6:1

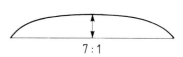

7:1

6. *Chord to Depth Ratios.* The top one at 4:1 is for a running spinnaker, flattening to 7:1 for a reacher.

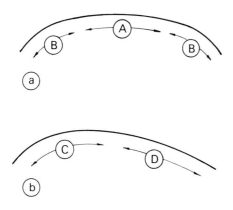

7. *Spinnaker Sections.* (a) When running, the middle A should be flatter than the shoulders at B. (b) When reaching, the flow should move towards the leading edge C. Ideally, the area of sail in the trailing edge D should flatten out, but the elasticity of nylon sometimes prevents this.

31

Spinnaker

Entry Curve. Having established the amount of camber or belly needed in the sail, we must now look at the way in which it takes up that horizontal section from the luff–the entry curve. The section should be an ellipse with a flattish middle section as shown in Fig 7, and this is the shape you should be looking for when running. As soon as you come onto a reach, the luff of the sail will take more weight so that it presents a flatter entry as indicated in Fig 7. On a reach the exit, or run-off for the wind, should if anything be flatter than the entry; this is to avoid backwinding the mainsail. Tension on the luff causes the leech to flatten, so see that the pole is down rather than up, and that the sheet does not pull too hard down on the leech to cause it to curl. Remember that the wind is blowing from luff to leech, so that both a free entry to the aerofoil section and a free exit become more important the closer to the wind you are sailing.

Roach

The roach is that portion of a sail outside the straight line joining two corners, which can be persuaded to set under normal use. With the spinnaker it can be divided into shoulders and skirt.

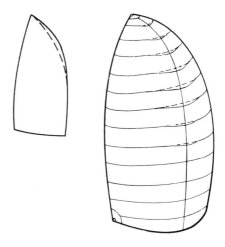

8. *'Roman Nose'.* Excessive centre fullness in the top of the spinnaker prevents the head opening properly and causes loss of drive.

Shoulders. The main point for debate as regards the head is how much shoulder should be built into the top half of the sail. The desire to make it as large as possible must be tempered by the knowledge that any extra material put there in the form of a roach has to be supported by the body of the sail. The broader the shoulders, the deeper must be the horizontal cross section – a lower chord to depth ratio. But we have already seen that this ratio is critical in that the deeper the sail, the less it wants to open up and present its area to the wind.

Part and parcel of the problem of shoulders is the vertical section of the sail, i.e. the depth measured in relation to a line taken from the head to the mid point of the sail (as opposed to the horizontal section); this is sometimes called the 'nose', so that a spinnaker with a pronounced vertical section at the head is said to have a 'Roman nose'.

The amount of roach at the shoulders will affect, and be affected by, the angle at the head when viewed from the front – in other words, how blunt the upper point of the sail is. Measured in terms of spherical geometry (assume that the head of the spinnaker is at the North Pole and that the sail spreads over the surface of the globe from there down), the head angle is the angle between the meridians formed by the two luffs. Angles will vary between a low of 60° for a narrow head storm spinnaker, through 75°–85° for star-cut and tri-radial sails, to 115° for the largest running spinnaker. As I say, these are based on spherical geometry, and are rather less than would be found by physical measuring of any particular spinnaker. If the angle is allowed to get too wide, either the shoulders are too broad or the nose too deep. In either case the luffs won't spread and stand in anything but a fresh breeze which is nearly dead aft.

Skirt. We have seen how any attempt to make extra large shoulders can do more harm than good, and the same applies to extending the area of the foot. You cannot simply hang more cloth on the bottom of the sail to catch the wind, for it has the effect of pulling the rest of the sail down; equally, as with large shoulders, a large skirt won't stand except with the wind aft. The optimum roach which can be added is about 12½ per cent of the foot length (1½in per foot), in other words a sail with a foot of 24 feet could usefully set a skirt three feet deep; one of 40 feet could take five feet.

Aspect Ratio

The scientific definition of aspect ratio takes account of a shape which is narrower at the top than the bottom; for a triangle it compares the height with half the width of the base (thus relating to the *average* width of the triangle throughout its height). To be precise with a spinnaker would be difficult due to its varying taper, so I shall simply relate luff to foot as being something easily identifiable. We shall see as we progress how the fore-triangle measurements affect the proportions of any spinnaker, particularly under the IOR rule, and it will be interesting to compare the sails produced by masthead and fractional rigs.

Tall narrow spinnakers are not particularly efficient sails, in that they do not trap much wind aloft, and they are often unstable because they tend to oscillate too much. We can classify under this heading all spinnakers which have a luff length more than double the width of the sail. Experience shows that 1·8:1 is about the maximum luff to foot ratio for a general purpose spinnaker.

Fore-triangle. The rule governing maximum luff and width means that a no-penalty IOR spinnaker of 1·8:1 needs to have an I:J ratio of about 3·3:1, so, we may conclude that a fore-triangle which is narrower than this in width for its height will produce an inefficient spinnaker. Within reason, the lower the ratio the more stable the spinnaker, so that proportions of luff to maximum width can be as broad as 1·5 or 1·4:1 in practice; under the IOR rule this sort of sail is produced by a fore-triangle ratio of 2·5:1 or thereabouts. As a matter of interest, some spinnakers for 12-metres and International 14 Footers, where width is unrestricted, have had a ratio of less than 1:1 and been successful sails.

Fractional v Masthead Rig

Let us now examine the pro's and con's of fractional and masthead rigs down wind. The most immediately apparent difference is in the size of their respective spinnakers relative to their mainsails. The fractional rig produces a better balance between mainsail and spinnaker, because the latter is smaller than the spinnaker of a masthead boat to the same rating. With the advent of lightweight hulls, sheer size has ceased to be an overriding factor, because optimum speed is quickly reached and it is more a matter of not heeling the boat too much or she will take up an inefficient underwater shape, with excessive drag and leeway. In addition, an oversize spinnaker will be more hidden behind its mainsail, so that a greater area is working in dead air and has to be supported by that part of the sail which is clear; shape is thus distorted and performance suffers accordingly. A further advantage of the smaller sail is that it is more easily controlled in a smart breeze, particularly during the gybe, and a chute furling system is more likely to be operable.

Rules change, so that during one period the mainsail may be favoured and during another it may be the fore-triangle which is encouraged. While mainsails are not being too heavily taxed, it pays at least to keep the proportion of sail aft of the mast relatively large; I don't think there will ever be a return to the situation where mainsails were almost token sails. This being so, the fractional rig has an advantage in the rating, as the following figures show. They are taken from some tests carried out by Messrs Camper & Nicholson in the late '70's between two sister ships

built to the Half-Ton rule (they were to the lines of *Silver Jubilee*), but one rigged masthead and the other ⅞ths. Based on an RSAT of 480 sq ft, the vital statistics of the two sail areas were as follows:

	masthead	⅞ths
I	38·5′	34·5′
J	11·6′	11·5′
P	32·65′	37·5′
E	10·0′	12·0′

It will quickly be seen that the fractional rig had an advantage in area while spinnakers were not being flown—as a matter of fact it works out at some five per cent. The spinnakers, however, reversed this difference, with the added advantage to the masthead boat that a blooper was not a practical proposition for the fractional rig because the large mainsail blanketed it. We won't go here into the advantage to be gained from the fractional rig's more easily bent mast, nor into the pro's and con's of the windward ability of the two rigs. Suffice it to say that a lightweight boat should profit handsomely from the bigger mainsail except in light winds, but that an increase in displacement of the yachts might make the choice marginal—which should make the average owner long for the more care-free life with the smaller spinnaker.

As I say, however, the rule can change all things. Back in 1960 the same firm built for the RORC rule two wooden 36 footers to the lines of their successful *Jolina*. One was masthead and the other ⅞ths rig, and the masthead boat won almost every time unless it was blowing really hard.

Within all this debate, the basic shape of the spinnaker remains the same; so does its control. We are thus left very much where we started, with a sail whose shape is the province of the sailmaker, but which has to be controlled by the crew. Other things being equal, does the owner really care?

Not if he is a racing man, no. All he wants is to understand his sails in order to get the most out of his boat. If he is a blue water sailor, he probably won't give house room to a spinnaker. So we are left with the coastal cruiser; he will probably accept the greater convenience of the smaller sail with open arms, and then keep it flying for too long as the wind gets up. You can't win.

Faults

There are sail faults which are the result of bad design and there are others which develop with use or misuse. It is those which come into the latter category with which we are chiefly concerned here.

It is easy to condemn a spinnaker roundly and out of hand but, if the matter is to be corrected, the sailmaker will need something more specific to go on; he will almost certainly want to see the sail set for himself, but much time can be saved if he has a reasonable idea of why you are dissatisfied. It is not easy for the layman to judge spinnaker shape and, as there are no absolute criteria with which to make a comparison, it can be difficult to assess the cause of trouble. One of the best ways is to obtain photographs of the sail, taken from off the boat if possible, but those taken from on board are better than nothing; try to get as much of the sail into the photograph as possible, so that reference may be made to whereabouts the trouble lies. Make use of sunlight to enhance shadows caused by wrinkles. A sailmaker can often spot the problem immediately from an intelligently taken photograph, where a long description will leave him none the wiser.

With more than any other sail, it must be remembered that a spinnaker has a large area of light cloth, into which it is not possible to design a lot of stability. It is very easy to overstress a light sail and so distort the shape built into it. Unfortunately it is not always possible to make good the damage caused by this sort of misuse.

If a spinnaker has given a good account of itself over a period of time, the most likely trouble spots are the luffs and the flow in the main body of the sail.

Luffs

Accurate shaping of the luffs is important, and one of the more frequent faults is that the tapes become tight. This will make the whole luff too tight, which causes it to turn in and, while this is not too serious on the run, it ruins the entry curve and thus the airflow as soon as the wind comes round towards the beam. The reason is not usually shrinkage of the luff tape but stretch of the nylon. The cure is for the sailmaker to remove the tapes and add a little extra length when he puts them back.

Because this is a predictable problem, sailmakers sew luff tapes rather slacker than is at first necessary, so that the cloth may stretch to match. The result is that, when new, these over-slack tapes will look wrinkled, and they will tend to flutter when the spinnaker is used in light airs. After the sail has been used once or twice in a breeze, it should stretch and settle down; if it does not, the sailmaker has miscalculated, and he should remove the tapes and adjust them.

In the past, spinnakers used to be made with wires in the luffs, indeed this was called for by some rules. The result was that the wires did not

37

7. *Opposite* The spinnaker is being allowed to fly too high, which opens the middle until it is nearly flat, thus losing drive. The sail has been made wider at some time, by the introduction of a bullet down the middle; apart from flattening the sail a bit too much, it seems to have worked well.

Hood Sailmakers

stretch at all but the sail did, so that all too often the sail had curling luffs.

As I have said above, therefore, the owner should beware of using his light weather spinnaker in winds too strong for it. If it doesn't blow out, the cloth may well stretch excessively and cause the problem we have seen. A tri-radial or star-cut sail resists these tensions which radiate from the corners better than one made with horizontal panels, which suffers the strains on the bias across the sailcloth so that it distorts and develops a middle aged spread.

A spinnaker will sometimes give the appearance of not wanting to open at the head and, although this can usually be attributed either to bad setting or original bad design, it can also be caused by the luff tapes being too tight. If the sail is developing a middle aged spread as described above, this will also tend to prevent the top of the sail from opening to the full.

If the fabric from which the sail is made is of good quality, however, it is possible for the sailmaker to take in some cloth across the sail and restore some of its original shape. The examination and subsequent adjustment is time consuming, and only worth while on a sail that is relatively new and where the cloth has a lot of stability left in it.

The Foot

The skirt is part of the sail which is perpetually under the owner's eye, and thus comes in for rather more than its fair share of criticism. Trouble usually comes in the form of slackness which causes it to flap, or failure to follow the contour of the body of the sail; the skirt of a full spinnaker may, however, curl up on a reach, particularly if the sheet is too far aft, but this is not of great consequence. Correction is possible but again it will require the sail to be set, and the attention of the sailmaker. It can often be cured by reshaping the centre seam at the foot of the sail or by the insertion of extra seams or darts in the foot.

Head Girts

If the spinnaker suffers from creases or girts running down from the head into the body of the sail, the shoulders are probably too wide to be properly supported. Some extra cloth has to be cut out of the head, and this is a job for the sailmaker. An alternative cause is that the middle of the sail is too flat, thus creating a difference between the curve in the two parts of the sail; the cure is once again removing cloth from the head to restore the balance.

Alterations

Altering the size of a spinnaker used to be a relatively easy job in the days when most of them were cut horizontally with a vertical centre seam.

Because the bottom half of the sail is virtually rectangular, a horizontal slice could be taken out or added at a seam somewhere above the clews; similarly the sail could be unpicked down the middle and a new vertical centre panel added, tapering to a point at the head, or else each half could have a vertical slice trimmed off before remaking the centre seam. None of these alterations necessitated tampering with the corners, which made things quick and easy.

But the star-cut has put an end to all that – at least if the owner wants to be left with a top racing spinnaker. Because the panels run at varying angles across the sail, alterations in size do not fit so conveniently into the pattern of things. It is surprising, however, what mistreatment the elastic nature of nylon can absorb, and quite a respectable cruising spinnaker will be left even after the knife has been wielded straight down the middle, cutting seams at whatever angle they happen to offer. When resewn as a smaller sail, there is a good chance that it will still set well enough for many people, despite the vertical slash; the same goes for shortening the luffs by taking out a horizontal strip. Even adding a panel seems to work, providing the owner is not too fussy about local wrinkles and bulges. But the racing man may think twice before he accepts such an alteration unless his pocket is particularly shallow.

Repairs

Most major repairs to a racing spinnaker are best left to a sailmaker, because the cloth is delicate and can easily be distorted into wrinkles by uneven stitching. But there are occasions when a perfectly good mending job can be done at home or even on board.

Small tears can be patched quite satisfactorily with proprietory repair tape, which comes in coloured nylon rolls two inches wide, with adhesive backing. When applying the tape, the sail must be held out under some tension on a smooth surface, using thumb tacks or map pins (which leave less marks in the surface) or, if you are working on the dining room table, weights. The idea is for the tape to be slightly slacker than the sail but, if the latter is not spread firmly, it will end up slacker than the tape – result, wrinkles. The sail must be dry and free from excessive salt; if the area to be patched is salty, wash it in fresh water and dry it thoroughly. Ideally the repair tape should follow the threadline of the sail, but this is by no means essential. Remove the protective paper and then press the tape down firmly; the harder you rub, the better it sticks, because friction produces heat, which helps ensure a good bond.

If the tear is of any size, the whole job may be sewn round with a machine after the tape is in place. Before doing so, it is wise to hold the sail out to make sure that the repair has not puckered or gathered the cloth at all. If two people hold it out between them, any creases will be quite obvious, and should be removed before getting to work with the sewing machine.

A common fault when an amateur mends a tear, is that he pulls it together too much. An edge torn along the threadline will have lost a number of the yarns which run parallel to the tear, so there will appear to be a small gap filled only by the frayed ends of the threads at right angles to the edge. These ends should not be more than butted together, or the sail will wrinkle. If the surface is pinned out under tension, the problem will be quickly apparent; do not be tempted to distort the sail to fill the gap.

If a hole has to be patched with a spare piece of cloth, somewhat more care is necessary and a sewing machine is virtually essential; double sided adhesive tape is useful here, as elsewhere in the repair kit. Patching is a specialist job, and some expertise is required, so don't start on your best racing sail. Buy a good book on the subject (*The Care and Repair of Sails* published by Adlard Coles Ltd in the UK and also by Sail Books in the USA), or take a few lessons from someone who knows dressmaking, and practise first on a piece of spare cloth or an old sail. Machining light cloth is not easy, and one of the most common faults is puckering due to excessive tension of the thread; another is failure to keep the new material lined up correctly, so that uneven stresses are set up. Don't be disappointed at early failure, because it is quite surprising what can be done with a seemingly irrepairable series of strips of nylon. But this requires space to lay out the sail and sort it all out, which in turn means a job best done by the sailmaker in his spacious loft–something which most of us will happily accept if things look that bad.

3

Spinnaker Gear

Mention has already been briefly made of the gear needed to set, trim and gybe a spinnaker. It is complex and varied, but an examination of the top ten boats in any fleet will reveal that the basic systems are not dissimilar. One of the most important points to remember is that whatever you choose should be well tried and race proven; there is no advantage in opting for something different when there is gear available which has stood the test of time.

This is not to say that development will not continue. But this is the kind of experimentation which is best left to those who are prepared for the expense and disappointment which such test work can often bring – if it should succeed, the innovator receives his reward in the shape of a coveted cup, but those who follow reap the benefit for all time, and at none of the development costs. Let us therefore be content with what we know to be right, both from the point of view of efficiency and simplicity.

The Pole

The spinnaker pole is the most basic piece of equipment needed to fly a chute. Its design is by no means uniform, indeed its construction is not critical and the method used to calculate its section for any particular boat is largely empirical. Apart from being a method of holding the tack apart from the clew, the pole has to respond to a number of other requirements. These are as follows:

(a) Lightness for ease of handling.
(b) Rigidity, and strength in compression.
(c) Ease of attachment to the mast, with universal movement.
(d) Height adjustment on the mast.
(e) Ease of attachment to the spinnaker tack.
(f) Control of vertical angle by the topping lift.
(g) Control of fore and aft angle by the fore and after guys.

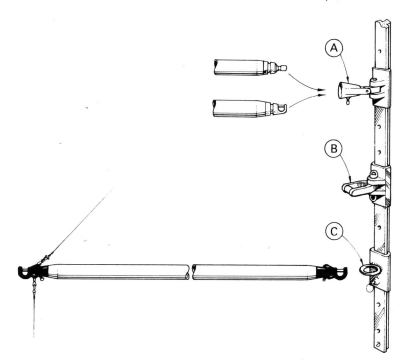

9. *Double-ended Spinnaker Pole.* The cup retains the pole by means of a lug which fits into a recessed ring in the tapered end. Alternatively the hook or clip on the pole may fasten to a strap across a hinged stirrup fitting, or to a simple ring fitted to the mast.

A = Cup.　B = Strap.　C = Plain ring.

Strength/Weight Ratio

A good strength to weight ratio is one of the most important factors, for not only must the spar be able to withstand the loadings put upon it, but it must also be easily handled by the foredeck crew; while not in use it is a dead weight which has to be carried on deck, usually forward. Various methods of reducing weight without sacrificing strength have been tried, including resort to carbon fibres. David May was one of the pioneers in this, when he tried them with his 1972 *Winsome* but, while the material was satisfactory in most respects, it failed under the side impact when it struck the forestay hard and repeatedly. Today a straightforward light alloy tube is accepted as being the most satisfactory material and, except on the larger boats, spinnaker poles are not usually tapered. *43*

8. Twin cups on Simplicity's single track are separated by a solid rod. Vertical adjustment is by a line.
Author

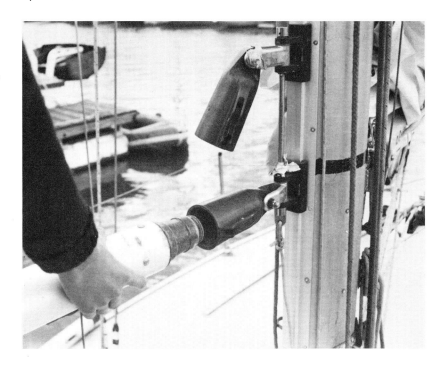

Mast Attachment

The spinnaker pole of our forefathers was supported on the mast by having a pair of jaws on its inner end, similar to those at the throat of a mainsail's gaff. The modern system, however, is to have either a ring onto which a piston plunger hook on the end of the pole can snap, or else a cup into which the whole end is fitted, with a catch to hold it in place. In both cases, the mast fitting is usually provided with some means of up and down adjustment, usually in the form of a slider held in place on a track by a spring loaded plunger. On large boats the loadings are large, so that some means must be provided to haul the slider up and down when it is under load. This may be a simple pulley, or else perhaps a form of winding gear comprising an endless belt attached to the gooseneck fitting. The pole end can be wound up or down by revolving the lower wheel with a winch handle. The belt may be either a rope or line gripped by grooved wheels or else a chain working on sprockets; see Fig 10. Where a boat uses two spinnaker poles for its gybe system, the mast fitting must also be duplicated, and this usually takes the form of two sliders held in tandem on a single track centrally placed; one sometimes finds two tracks side by side, each carrying its own slider, but this brings the need to use the correct track with each pole, and it makes single pole dip gybing impossible should one pole be broken.

44

The fittings at either end of the pole may be different where a dip pole system is used, otherwise the two ends should be the same, so that each may fasten either into the ring or cup on the mast, and also onto the spinnaker guy or brace. A typical double acting fitting is shown at Fig 9.

The Gooseneck System
As with the pole itself, the means by which it is attached to the mast, the gooseneck system, must respond to certain requirements.

(a) It must act as a universal joint, capable of swinging in any direction.
(b) It must be easy to ship and unship.
(c) In many cases it must also be capable of attaching to the spinnaker guy.
(d) There should be some system of remote control, so that the retaining catch or plunger can be tripped from anywhere along the pole.
(e) The system must be able to accept loadings in both sheer and thrust as well, at times, as tension.

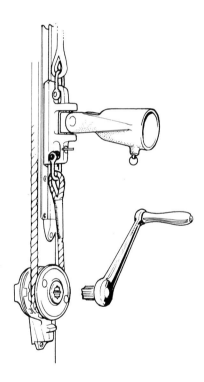

10. *Pole Height Crank.* The inner end of the spinnaker pole may be raised or lowered through cranking the slider up or down the track on the mast by means of a rope or chain drive.

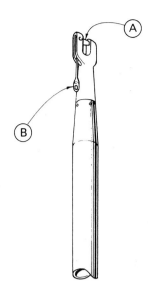

11. *Fork Attachment.* The pole end may be in the form of a flattened fork, which attaches to a stirrup as in Fig 9, or to a simple fixed ring.

A = Retaining catch, spring-loaded, opens inwards so it may be snapped over ring or strap.

B = Lever to open catch for release.

The system most commonly used on small boats is the piston hook and ring, while boats above 25–30 feet overall or those which race seriously use the cup and socket. The former is cheap and simple, but can suffer from lack of strength and a tendency to lock under certain conditions because it is not fully universal in its action, but we shall see below that it has been used at quite high levels of competition. The cup and socket can be made strong and fully universal. It consists of a cup into which the end of the pole fits and is retained by a spring loaded plunger engaging into a groove cut round the cone on the end fitting. This permits the pole to revolve around its longitudinal axis, thus eliminating torque loads. Its main drawback is that the cups on the mast track are somewhat large and clumsy, but this is really only one of aesthetics: they seem clumsy because they are free to flop about; a winch is bigger and less finely built, but it is not considered clumsy because it is fixed in one position.

An alternative is the flattened fork, which is attached to the mast so that its opening is arranged vertically; there is a horizontal retaining pin. The end of the pole is similarly flattened, so that it can be inserted into the fork, located by the horizontal pin and retained by a spring loaded catch. As the pole can pivot up and down on this pin, it is only necessary for the fork to pivot horizontally for the universal joint to be complete.

The reverse of the cup type fitting, where the gooseneck consists of a universally jointed spigot which fits inside a hollow cone in the end of the pole, was used a few years ago by at least one spar maker. It never became popular and is now rarely seen, probably because mating of the two fittings is more difficult, and it was too easy to trap one's fingers; foredeck hands without fingers are none too handy.

Simplicity

Simplicity and efficiency often go hand in hand; they are also often accompanied by economy. The piston hook on the end of the pole which attaches to a ring on the mast is simple, and may be used on boats up to about 30 feet long. The engineering needs to be robust in order to support the thrust loads likely to be encountered, but I have used the ring and hook on three of my Half-Tonners with perfect success.

On one boat I used an idea copied from Doug Gilling's *September* when he brought her over for the Captain Cook Trophy. Doug had done away with the track up the front of the mast and replaced it with three permanently fixed eyes. The top one was as high as could be comfortably reached above the deck, the bottom one was low enough for use with a star-cut spinnaker, and the third was half way between. In three seasons using the same system on my *Timbalina* I never had cause to find fault. I am not saying that it might not be a bit crude on a boat contesting the World's Half-Ton cup today but, for the owner not so interested in that sort of racing, it is an admirable way of saving money.

9.   The wire guy is rove to run freely through the plunger fitting, and then snaps onto a ring on the sheet's snap shackle, which in turn attaches to the clew.

Author

Outer End

The outer end fitting is designed to keep the tack of the spinnaker in place. In the old days this became simply a matter of clipping the sail to the pole, and large grommets were worked into the corners so that this could be done; the guy was also attached to the sail of course. In practical terms the pole could not be separated from the sail and guy without much difficult handling, and all this made gybing unnecessarily difficult. It is the practice today to keep the guy and sheet fastened to the sail, and arrange matters so that the guy runs through a fitting on the end of the pole. A special outhaul has been used to achieve this, passing from the corner of the sail, through the end fitting and back along the boom where it could be made fast. To assist in gybing, this line was sometimes led to the other clew. A bell-like end fitting was designed so that the outhaul could pass internally along the pole; in the case of twin   47 poles, each had such an outhaul which could be used to draw the pole end to the appropriate corner of the spinnaker. This was later modified so that the end fitting was loose on a wire which passed down the inside of the pole; the fitting was clipped onto the guy anywhere along its length, and then pulled into the bell mouth at the outer end of the pole.

The system was popular for a time, but has given way to the older fixed piston plunger fitting. This plunger is usually held closed by a spring, and can be opened by a line along the pole; sometimes there is a catch to hold it open, with a trigger in the jaws which is actuated by pressure from the guy or brace once it is snared. Be careful, because the spring is usually powerful, and hand triggering by mistake could cost you a finger or two; jaws is the correct word to use here.

Once the guy is located in the end fitting, the pole slides up it to the tack, helped if necessary by pulling on the foreguy. I have seen this even further simplified: the fitting of John Tyler's *Sprinter* was a fixed eye through which the guy was permanently rove; because this could not switch sides, it was of course necessary always to use the twin pole gybe system.

The piston plunger fitting has several advantages. First, on smaller boats particularly, the same fitting may be used at each end of the pole; as can be seen in the chapter on gybing, this can be a help. On larger boats things become more sophisticated, so that this type of fitting cannot always be used on the inner end. Secondly, the piston plunger usually has a collar which is free to revolve around the piston. When the guy is being pulled through the fitting, the collar rotates and prevents the piston being opened accidently—a problem which can occur without this refinement. Thirdly, we have already mentioned the remotely operated tripping line to open the piston from the inner end.

Self Stowing Lifts
It saves time if the topping lift can be permanently attached to the outer end of the pole, but it would obviously be very much in the way if no special provision were made. To simplify matters, let us assume that the pole is stowed as far forward as possible on the foredeck, with its inner end close by the chain plates. The essence of the idea is that the lift is fastened to the outer (or forward) end of the pole in the normal way, and is then run back along the top of the pole to a hook of some sort low down, whence it can go to its sheave up the mast, lying close to the shrouds and out of the way. There are two ways of retaining the lift in this position so that it is ready for immediate use. The first is with a snap hook, which is fastened either to the spinnaker pole itself or low down in the rigging. The former is preferable, as the lift may still be kept out of the way when the pole is attached to the mast, which can be an advantage if one has to tack with a jib set just prior to hoisting the spinnaker.

48   The second method is to use shock cord elastic, which is snapped to

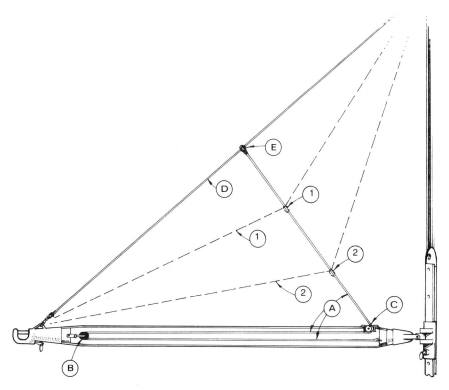

12. *Self-stowing Lift.* As the lift D is slackened, the stretched shock-cord A shortens and draws the lift down to the exit box C, so that the lift lies close along the spinnaker pole and up the mast.

A = Shock-cord elastic.   B = Pulley.
C = Exit box and sheave.   D = Pole lift.
E = Ring or snap hook on end of shock-cord.
1 and 2 = Intermediate positions.

the topping lift to draw it down to the inner end of the pole when it is not under tension. The elastic has to be very long to be able to stretch right out and allow the topping lift to straighten when in use, so that some form of stowage inside the pole is needed (see Fig 12).

Finally the bottom part of the lift may be formed by a wire span. This is just long enough to reach along the top of the pole back to the inner end, where it is spliced to a ring. The lift proper is clipped to the ring, as is the shock cord stowage or else a Swedish hank to hold it down to the pole.

The spinnaker pole is subject to measurement under most rules, and this is discussed elsewhere.

10. The jockey pole may be held fore and aft by a lashing on the shrouds. The pole here is not, of course, under load so it is resting on the lifeline.

Author

Jockey Pole or Reaching Strut

When a spinnaker is used on a close reach, the pole must be eased well forward or the sail will not set. This means that the brace or guy leads progressively nearer the fore and aft line of the boat until eventually it bears on the shrouds. Apart from chafing the rope itself, this results in a highly inefficient angle as regards purchase on the pole when it has to be pulled aft. The cure to both these problems lies in the reaching strut.

Clipped to the mast, usually by means of a piston hook to a fixed ring, the jockey pole has an open fork with a roller at the other end, which is engaged in the guy so as to push it outboard clear of the shrouds; this gives it a better mechanical advantage on the end of the spinnaker pole. If there are not two shrouds conveniently close together between which the reaching strut may pass, it is usual to lash it to one of the main shrouds with a sail tie to prevent it swinging forward or aft; some up and down movement may be accepted, indeed it is necessary. Attachment may also be made by means of a metal hook near the outer end of the reaching strut. To rig the strut, the hook is clipped over the shroud and the inner end is levered onto the mast ring. This has the advantage that the hook may be used as a fulcrum to lever the guy out if, as so often happens, the strut must be fitted after the load has come on the guy with a shy spinnaker.

I have often been surprised at the little thought given by some owners to the proper arrangement of this simple device. It must not be fastened too high up the mast, or it will not lie at right angles to the plane of the spinnaker guy when this is at full stretch. If it is not at right angles, the load will not be in true compression, so that the strut can be distorted or even broken. The correct position may be easily assessed at moorings by rigging the guy or brace in the spinnaker pole and allowing it to take up its usual angle when on a close reach; pole height and guy fairlead should be correct, of course, and then the arrangement of the reaching strut will become obvious.

Halyard

The spinnaker halyard is not really very different from a halyard that pulls up any variety of other sails – or is it? Compared with its close relative the jib halyard, it has to cope with somewhat different circumstances.

The jib halyard is under constant load from a constant direction. The spinnaker halyard, on the other hand, is liable to be pulled in a variety of directions with uneven loadings. When the spinnaker collapses and refills with a bang, some of the shock will be passed to the halyard, which must be capable of absorbing it both in tension and direction. Not only must the halyard itself cope with this, but the design of the whole masthead fitting has to be such that it can withstand side loads, torsion and shear.

The pull can vary through a vertical arc from just above the horizontal to nearly straight down; it is also liable to come from either side from one beam to the other. To cover this range and to allow the sail to be gybed from one side to the other, the mast sheave must be fitted above the highest forestay attachment. Most racing rules have something to say about positioning this sheave, and it must usually be as close as practical to the point where the forestay joins the mast.

A racing boat of any size or seriousness has to have two spinnaker halyards to enable peels or quick changes to be effected. They are usually run through sheaves sited side by side just above the forestay, so that care has to be exercised not to get the leads crossed (hence the need to peel inside or outside, depending on which is the spare halyard, as described in Chapter 8). The small keelboat and the cruising man will usually only have one spinnaker halyard, from a centrally mounted sheave either shackled onto the crane which projects forward from the masthead, or else recessed into it. The hauling part of the halyard is often taken down outside the mast rather than internally like that for a mainsail or jib, largely because hoisting is quicker if the whole thing is free from any restriction – and speed in getting a spinnaker up is often important. If the halyard is internal, the exit should be well up the mast, using a turning block on deck if necessary, to ease hoisting problems.

There is controversy as to whether a spinnaker halyard should be wire or rope on large boats. If you have a modern racing mast with three halyards, two of which may be used for either the spinnaker or the genoa, these must meet the more stringent needs of the genoa and should therefore be of wire with rope tails. If you have one or two halyards specifically for hoisting the spinnaker, they are best if made entirely of rope, which should be braided because it will not twist under load. The deciding factor is one of shock absorption: a rope halyard absorbs shock loadings better than one made of wire.

When the spinnaker is set shy, the lead at the head of the halyard will be abeam, so that the wise owner will keep an eye open for chafe where the same bit of rope pulls sideways from the sheave casing. A single pulley shackled with a swivel attachment will take up the correct line, but recessed sheaves have no such adjustment, and their casings should be belled outwards so as to avoid this problem.

The strongest argument against an all rope halyard, therefore, is that it can chafe. If the trouble is persistent, I would suggest a composite halyard, having six to ten feet of wire at the top end to withstand this trouble. Back in the 'seventies the well known British offshore racer *Quailo* had internal spinnaker halyards at one time, and experienced chafe from fittings inside the mast, so they had to increase the length of wire to thirty or forty feet.

The Head Swivel

A swivel always used to be fitted to the head of a spinnaker; indeed, some sailmakers still fit one, but it is more normally omitted unless specifically ordered by the owner. This is because the swivel is now-adays contained within the halyard's own snap shackle, so there is no need to carry the extra weight aloft—apart from the fact that spinnaker swivels are both difficult to obtain and very expensive. When Ratsey's were asked to fit one to the head of a storm spinnaker for the 90ft *Gitana IV*, they were lucky enough to find the remains of an old cotton spinnaker they had made in the 'thirties for the royal yacht *Britannia*, still with its immensely strong bronze swivel.

The job of the swivel, as we have already seen, is two-fold. First, it allows the sail to untwist should there have been any faulty packing; secondly, any laid rope or wire will tend to untwist with the lay as it is pulled, so that this must be allowed to work itself out by means of the swivel.

Guys/Braces

Regardless of the gybing system employed, or how the guys or braces are rigged, the latter have one prime requirement: they must not stretch. If they do, the pole will move about and alter the coarse trim of the spinnaker so that it may collapse; if the guy stretches when close reaching, the pole can swing forward so that the weight is taken sideways on the forestay, with consequent danger to the deck fitting.

How then can we see that the guy does not stretch? The first material which comes to mind is wire, and this can often be found on larger boats—with, of course, a rope tail so that it may be handled by the crew more readily. The splice joining the rope and the wire needs to be carefully positioned so that the crew is never required to pull on wire, even when the pole is right aft and the brace short; equally, it is desirable that as much wire as possible be incorporated, so that there is little stretch when the pole is right forward. At all events, the splice must be carefully served to prevent gashers of wire strands tearing into hands.

I have before now gone to the trouble to extract the core from a braided rope and replaced it with wire but, while giving an excellent result, this is a cumbersome process and fortunately there is some extremely good non-stretch braided line on the market these days. Developed in Germany, this consists of a Kevlar core with a braided sheath; the latter may be removed if the sheaves will not take the bulk, without loss of strength when compared with wire; some outer cover should be left at the tail for ease of handling. Gleistein is a good example of this, and it can even have snap shackles swaged on the end.

Foreguys/Downhauls

The foreguy or downhaul is short enough not to stretch so much that pole trim can be upset, provided the rope is not nylon (which stretches a lot) and is stout enough. Use polyester pre-stretched three-strand rope if you can't afford Gleistein. It must reach from the outer end of the pole when squared off, to the bow and back to the cockpit or point where it will be handled. Allow something extra because the foredeck hand will need some slack at the bow in the process of sail handling.

Sheets

Spinnaker sheets may be allowed some stretch, because they control the fine trim and any elongation will not affect the basic trim of the sail—indeed, a puff of wind may sometimes require the sheet to be eased slightly, which can be effected by a little stretch. Here again, plenty of length is required, as the trimmer will often need to stand by the weather shrouds. If you cannot run a line on the boat herself, allow twice her overall length and you won't be far out.

Ghosting conditions require minimum weight on the free corner of the spinnaker, so a light line should be ready to tie to the clew after the sheet and guy have been removed.

Topping Lift

The last control for the spinnaker is the topping lift, often shortened simply to the lift or pole lift. The higher up the mast it is taken the better from the leverage point of view; the upper spreaders of a double spreader rig is high enough, but for a single spreader rig this point is too low and the sheave should be two thirds up. The lift must be long enough to run from the pole end back along the pole to the mast before going up to the sheave and down again; this is so that the boat may be tacked with the genoa set and the pole rigged for the spinnaker hoist, as already described under *Self-Stowing Lifts* above.

Except in small boats, the lift should be attached to the outer end of the pole, or else cross tensions will be set up by the downhaul and afterguy pulling on the end and the lift pulling in the middle. If an end-for-end gybing system is used, it is useful to be able to attach the lift and downhaul in the middle; this is best achieved by means of a bridle or span running the length of the pole, with an attachment point in the middle. The load is then transmitted to each end.

If the boat is big enough to need a wire topping lift, the wire to rope splice may be placed so that the splice is somewhere up the mast when being used to hold the spinnaker pole in place; if it is doubling as a staysail halyard, the wire should reach the winch when the sail is fully hoisted.

Where twin topping lifts are used for twin poles, it is a good tip not to have them emerging from the mast too close together, nor to use a sister block shackled to one point; if they are spaced a foot or so apart vertically and colour coded for identification, foredeck work will be much easier.

Terminals

The sheet is attached to the spinnaker by a swivel snap shackle, which should be one of those capable of being opened under load, whereas the one for the halyard should only open when the load is off (a matter of the location of the hinge). Snap shackles should have a tripping line for use by cold fingers, but do not put a loop in it in case it snags and releases inadvertently.

So that the guy may be released independently, it should be attached to a ring on the end of the sheet. There should be some form of stop on the guy to prevent the snap shackle or its splice from being hauled right into the end fitting of the spinnaker pole. This may take the form of a solid rubber or plastic ball, a disc of the same materials or, if you have the patience, a turk's head worked into the guy itself (assuming that you are using three strand laid rope). I picked up my most effective stop in a boatyard I was walking through. A hull under construction had been drilled with a circular saw toothed cutter to take a skin fitting, and there lying on the ground was the disc of fibreglass which had been cut out. It was about two inches in diameter, half an inch thick, and with a hole already drilled through the middle. Every boatbuilder throws hundreds of these away each year, so now you know.

Bags and Turtles

There are probably nearly as many different designs of turtles for spinnakers as there are people using them, or certainly as many as sailmakers producing them. Many of these only differ from one another in detail so, rather than list all the variations, I propose examining the requirements.

However it is packed, the spinnaker must come out cleanly and without twists. It therefore follows that an important consideration is that the turtle shall be of sufficient capacity for, if it is too small, the sail will most likely come out in one tight bundle, either to fill prematurely or else to fall as a lump into the water—possibly both. It must also have an opening big enough not to delay exit; use of a metal or plastic rim of some kind will help.

The turtle must be easily portable, so that it can be quickly taken on deck for hoisting. When it is in position, the head and clews of the spinnaker must be accessible for attachment of the halyard, sheets and guys but, at the same time, the body of the sail must be safely retained; there should be a means of clipping the turtle to the boat so that it is not lost overboard on hoisting.

There are two principal solutions to the problem. One takes the form of a sailbag, rather more squat than the normal tall bag, fitted with a solid hoop at the top and a lid or flaps to secure the sail. The other is box shaped, with the lid in the form of flaps held together by velcro and safety ties. There are usually three cut-outs in these flaps so that the head and clews may protrude.

Having said that, I have seen plastic trash cans, laundry baskets and even cardboard boxes used successfully. Whatever the form, it is important that waterproof material is not used for the turtle, as this will be found to keep more water in than out; in any case, see that a drain hole is fitted at the bottom and that it has a security line.

11.   The rope sheet has a centre-hinged snap shackle (also shown in Plate 9) so it can open under load; the rings allow the guy to be snapped to them easily. The snap shackle on the wire guy has a side hinge, and a circular stop to prevent the eye jamming in the pole end fitting. Note the knots in the lanyard on the sheet snap shackle—these not only give a good grip, but avoid too large a loop which could catch in obstructions.

Author

Deck Layout

The way in which the various pieces of equipment are arranged throughout the boat have an important bearing on the ease and speed with which sails are handled. The subject is sufficiently important to have its own book, and readers who wish to learn more about it are referred to *Designed to Win* by Roger Marshall. I propose here to list some of the reasoning which goes into laying out spinnaker gear, without examining the design process.

The essence of good layout is that everything shall come to hand easily and logically, by day and by night. Simple things like winches and cleats being correctly positioned make a world of difference.

12. *Sharp End Detail.* Visible are: the vertical pull of the downhaul via (twin) fairleads on the deck which can double as cunningham adjuster leads, genoa tack hooks, the feeder for groove luff headsails, the central deck track for setting staysails, and anti-chafe on the lifeline terminals.

Author

Sheet Winches

Sheet winches should be at a convenient height and distance for cranking, and the handle should move the full circle without danger to knuckles or the crewman next door. The angle between the upright axis of the winch and the sheet or halyard concerned as it arrives at the drum should be at least 95 degrees, or riding turns will build up; this can be achieved by use of turning blocks or a wedge shaped pad under the winch base to tilt it.

Winches form the backbone of any gear handling, and it is unwise to try to economise by buying winches which are not man enough for the job. It is better to have two good ones rather than four underpowered ones, even though it means working the headsail and spinnaker from the same winch, with the attendant problems of transferring sheets. If you are adding new winches, make sure that all handles are interchangeable.

Halyard Winches

One of the basic points of deck layout is whether the halyards should lead aft to winches amidships or at the forward end of the cockpit, or whether the winches should be on or around the mast. Both arrangements have their points, and I prefer to have control in the cockpit. But the spinnaker halyard winch is often best left on the mast, whichever system is used, because speed and control are better if the halyard doesn't lead half way round the boat before it gets to its winch.

Cleats

A cleat should always obey two rules. First, it should be on the opposite side of its winch to the direction from which the sheet or halyard arrives, as this evens out the pull on the winch. Secondly, it should be correctly angled to accept the rope concerned: clam cleats should be in a straight line, with the lead slightly up to the cleat so that the rope doesn't pull out upwards; horn cleats should make an angle of 15–20 degrees open with the winch, so that the sheet or halyard doesn't have to cross itself on the first turn. See Fig 13.

Jammers.   After exploding on the scene in the early 'seventies, sheet jammers have lost some of their early popularity. They have their uses for locking off a sheet or halyard in order to free the winch, but they tend to chew up the rope in the process. They can save the expense of another winch, but they aren't altogether cheap themselves, so think carefully before adopting them.

Sheet Lead

Just like a jib, a spinnaker requires an accurately placed sheeting point. Because there is such a long length of sheet between the fairlead and the

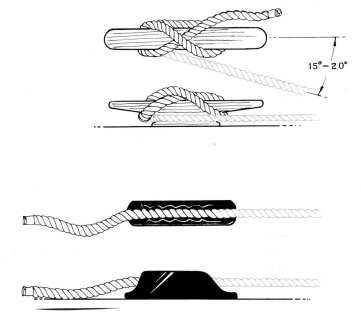

13. *Cleats.* A regular horn cleat requires the sheet or line to be led in at an open angle of 15°–20° so that it does not jamb the turns on the cleat. A clam cleat requires a straight lead.

sail, the position is not so critical as with a jib, where the clew is often only inches from the fairlead.

Many boats have their spinnaker sheeted to the counter, but the furthest aft this need really be taken is the length of the spinnaker pole aft of the mast. If you have a track on the rail, or the toe-rail has holes for fixing blocks, mark this position as the furthest aft you need to go; there should be facility to take the block forward, almost up to the chainplates. This would be necessary if you are setting a spinnaker with a foot and maximum width shorter than 180 per cent of SPL, or when on a dead run to clear the sheet from fouling the main boom, or to give a better shape on a reach or in heavy weather.

Guy/Brace Lead

If the boat has double sheets and guys, the best lead for the latter is forward of the sheet where the boat develops its maximum beam. In most boats this is just forward of the cockpit in the midships area. Unlike the sheet, there should be no need to alter the lead of the brace while sailing.

If the sheet becomes the guy in gybing, it will be useful to bring the lead further forward. This can be achieved by the strategic siting of a snatch block to take the guy, or else by barberhauling the lead downwards. The latter method has become very popular on small boats. The barberhauler is permanently fitted, and has a metal or plastic thimble in its end through which the sheet/guy can render freely. When not in use, it is left slack and the sheet can lead as it may; as soon as it is necessary to have the lead further forward, the barberhauler can be quickly brought into action.

Foreguy Lead

The foreguys are best led so as to give a pull straight down from the outer end of the spinnaker pole, to give the best mechanical advantage when it is right forward. It is customary to use blocks sited alongside the genoa tack fitting, but there is no reason why deadeye fairleads should not be used on boats up to about 35ft overall; these points can double as useful anchorages for headsail cunningham tackles. The foreguy will lead aft through turning blocks or intermediate deadeyes, so as to end near the after guy; these two usually have to be worked in concert, so they should be next to each other.

Topping Lift Lead

Here again this may be brought aft, close to the foreguy, because the two work together. But the need to alter the lift is not so frequent that the control has to come to the cockpit, and many boats leave it at the mast. The strongest argument for bringing it aft is on small craft, where movement or weight forward is bad for performance.

Halyard Stowage

It is quite common for a sloop to have seven halyards: mainsail, two genoa, two spinnaker and two topping lift. So some thought should be given to their stowage.

When the boat is at her berth, some of them may be taken to the rail or pulpit, clear of the mast, so that they do not inconvenience those sleeping aboard or near at hand by slatting on the mast. But while sailing they all need to come to hand quickly and surely, which usually means that the hauling and running parts must be near the heel of the mast – the running part of the spinnaker halyards may be taken to the pulpit. This is not good from a windage point of view, but it makes clearing the halyard prior to hoisting much easier. Moving the halyard from the heel of the mast to the pulpit could be part of the preparations for hoisting the spinnaker.

So, the main halyard aside, six separate points should be provided for the running parts. On two of my own boats I used a short length of alloy toe-rail with half a dozen holes drilled in it. This was bolted to the deck athwartships immediately in front of the mast, so that each halyard could be snapped on. Failing a special fitting, make sure that there is some suitable provision – the chainplates may even be used on some deck layouts.

13.   A convenient halyard stowage fitted at the foot of the mast.

Author

The hauling parts either emerge from the mast via sheave boxes, or else come down outside the mast (in the case of some spinnaker halyards). If they are worked from beside the mast, they should each have their own cleat, angled to the appropriate winch; if they pass via a turning block to a winch on deck, either just aft of the mast or nearer to the cockpit, they then clear the bottleneck, but should still be made off on a cleat sited by the winch concerned. With as many as six halyards, it is a good idea to code them. If your spinnaker halyards are rope, they will be obvious but a port and starboard identification will be helpful, likewise with genoa halyards and pole lifts; coloured adhesive tape is admirable for this purpose. Some owners also use a braille-type code for night sailing. While I am on the subject of identifying halyards, don't forget the fall of the pole lift, which may be marked to ensure that the correct slack is given for a smooth dip pole gybe.

Complementary Sails

It would be quite wrong to consider the spinnaker in isolation, for there are sails which can be used with it to improve speed and stability down wind. It should be borne in mind that there are two objects of such complementary sails. The first is to improve the airflow by forming a better slot between the spinnaker and the mainsail, and the second is to add area where it is best suited to the balance of the boat.

Blooper

This sail has been given a number of names. Many people know it as the 'Big Boy', but unfortunately this name is used in some parts of the world for a reaching staysail set under a spinnaker or high clewed reacher. Hoods call it a 'Shooter', but I recognise that this is a minority opinion and can also be confused with Ratsey's 'Shooting Star' spinnaker. So I shall conform to widespread practice and call it the 'Blooper' in this book.

The sail first hit the headlines in the 1971/72 Southern Cross series. Chris Bouzaid, the New Zealand sailmaker, flew his light genoa to leeward of the spinnaker in the now accepted manner of the blooper. This was much to the surprise of the other competitors, and a protest was lodged by the British team – largely to get an official ruling on the legality of the sail. They lost, with the result that the sail had made its mark on the racing scene. As with many innovations, however, this was not the first time it had been done. I remember seeing a photograph of *Vendetta* using her genoa in just this manner at Burnham off the east coast of England when I worked for Cranfield & Carter back in the 1960's, and I don't doubt that there is someone somewhere who could antedate this if we looked hard enough. But its use in such a prestigious series as the Southern Cross, and the hoo-ha of the protest, ensured that this time it was brought to everyone's attention. The blooper had arrived.

At this period virtually all but small boats were masthead rig. These

14. (a) *Study in Red, White and Blue* The helmsman of the Dutch *Anne Mazurka* must find it harder to see ahead than his rival in *SVWS* from Germany. The wind is nicely on the port quarter, so most of this 2-Ton Cup fleet are flying bloopers.

Alastair Black

14. (b) *Study in Green.* This Irish Helmsman won't see much. The boat
right aft on the other gybe shows that they are dead before the wind, so the
blooper is probably more of a hindrance than a help.

Alastair Black   *63*

rigs were growing taller and taller and, as a result, they were becoming more and more unstable down wind, because their spinnakers were becoming bigger and their mainsails taller and narrower. When on a fairly broad run, therefore, the large area of the spinnaker poled out to windward was out of balance with the much smaller mainsail to leeward. The essence of the blooper is to add area to leeward to redress this imbalance.

To give an example, take a typical masthead rigged One-Tonner. The mainsail has an area of about 300 sq ft, while the spinnaker set on the other side of the boat may have as much as 1300 sq ft. No wonder the boat is unbalanced and difficult to steer. Add the blooper, which has an area of about 600 sq ft, on the side of the mainsail and the rig is brought back into better balance. With easier steering and the extra sail area given by the blooper, more boat speed will result.

With the larger mainsail and smaller spinnaker carried on boats with fractional rig, the blooper has been found less necessary. The large mainsail not only blankets the blooper but, with the lower rig and smaller spinnaker, the down wind sailplan is not so out of balance. Another factor which makes the sail less necessary in this kind of boat, is that the mast is a lot further forward than with the masthead rig.

Under IOR conditions, the new sail counts as a jib and it has to comply with the rule on headsail size. But there is enough scope to produce a sail which works well.

Because we want to shift the centre of effort to leeward, it stands to reason that a blooper should be set with a slack halyard to allow it to sag well away from the spinnaker. It was quickly found that, in order to get the sail as far out to leeward as possible to catch the wind outside the leech of the mainsail, the luff of the blooper has to be hollowed very heavily— over three feet on a 45ft luff. This has two advantages, of which the first is to allow the sail to 'banana' out around the lee of the mainsail. The second is that, because of the rule governing the maximum half-height measurement of a genoa, this hollow in the luff allows the sailmaker to build a large roach onto the leech, thereby placing even more area to leeward. There have even been successful bloopers with a pronounced notch in the luff, as sailmakers struggled to maintain maximum area within the rule.

The sail is cut very full, especially at the head, to make it stable; it should have maximum foot roach. This shape is achieved almost entirely by panel shaping throughout the sail and, given a stable cloth, there is little reason to depart from a simple horizontal arrangement of the panels, although radial corners are used by some sailmakers. The result is a very full specialist sail which, with its enormous hollow in the luff, cannot be set with a tight halyard and so will not double up as a light headsail.

Because they are only used with the wind aft, most bloopers are made from the same weight of material as the regular running spinnaker, namely ¾oz nylon, but yachts taking part in long distance ocean racing often carry a second blooper of heavier cloth to use in the more arduous conditions encountered in open waters. Although a special shape has developed, if there is no purpose-made sail aboard, there is no reason why an existing genoa cannot be pressed into service as a blooper, as was done originally. A light genoa or a high clewed reacher can be successful, albeit demanding a bit more attention than the proper job.

Handling

Because it is an easy sail to set and douse (it all happens in the lee of the mainsail), and because it adds impressively to area, the blooper is popular with crews. It does, however, detract from forward visibility, so the skipper should not let enthusiasm run away with things, or the helmsman will be perpetually blind forward. We shall also see that wind conditions have to be right for the sail to pay dividends.

Hoisting. The tack has to go to the same tacking point as the genoa, for the blooper is a full LP sail; however, a tack strop 30in (0.76m) long is permitted. This is desirable as it helps get the area as far to leeward as possible. The sail does not have to pass over the top of the lifeline, and a better set is obtained if the tack strop is allowed to lead under the guardwire to the tacking point. It is advisable to use a snap shackle at the tack, for there is a fair chance of a loop coming off the modern type of tack hook.

The clew is controlled by a sheet which should lead as far aft as possible, and I always recommend that this should be kept attached and stowed away with the sail after use; it may be quite light and about one and a half times the boat's length. This sheet should, of course, be led outside everything and, as bloopers can pull very hard, the assistance of a winch may be necessary. To set the sail, it is hoisted to leeward, on either a genoa or spinnaker halyard, whichever is available. This halyard must be passed over and outside the spinnaker sheet and lazy guy so that the sail is pulled up outside them. The sail is pulled to about 80 per cent of the way up the mast and given plenty of sheet. The mainsail may be pulled in temporarily if necessary to assist the blooper to fill with wind.

The Wrap. In the unlikely event of the blooper getting into a wrap when being hoisted, it can usually be untwisted by hauling hard up on the halyard and pulling in on the sheet.

Trimming. Because the blooper shares with the spinnaker the dubious quality that it has no spars or stay to support it, it follows that there must be sufficient air flowing correctly across the sail to cause it to fill and stand. It sets to leeward of everything and, contrary to what might be

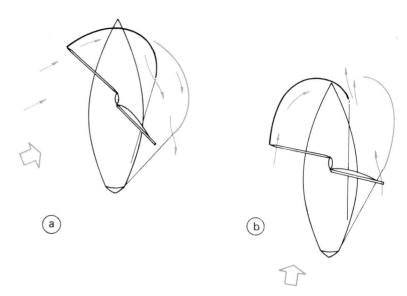

14. *Blooper Trim 1.* In (a) the wind is too far forward and passes over the blooper from forward to aft, bellying the leech and slowing down the boat. In (b) the wind is just off the weather quarter and gives correct flow forward in the blooper.

expected, the wind enters the sail at the leech and leaves at the luff. This is why it is important to have a large gap between the blooper and the spinnaker, if the airflow over the latter is not to be disturbed. It is also the reason for setting the sail as far out to leeward as possible: the wind goes into its leech from leeward of the mainsail.

These factors bring with them several problems. First, there must be sufficient wind speed to lift the sail – 7 or 8 knots over the deck is about the minimum, except in certain circumstances as we shall see later. Secondly, if the wind is too far aft, the blooper will set forwards rather than slightly sideways, thus getting into the wind shadow of the mainsail; the wind needs to be no closer to dead aft than 10 degrees. Thirdly, if the wind is too far towards the beam, it will not be able to get round the outside of the mainsail and into the blooper leech, but will go in between the mainsail luff and the blooper, thus trying to reverse the flow we want to establish; anything nearer to the beam than 50 degrees will cause this trouble. If this reverse reaching flow is allowed to establish itself, the fullness of the sail and the way it is set will, in fact, try to pull the boat backwards as the diagram shows. We thus have an arc of 40 degrees apparent wind in which the blooper will be effective.

Both the halyard and the sheet are used in trimming, and the former should be well eased to allow the sail to set close to the water. This gets it away from the boat and out from behind the mainsail but, most important, gives a good sized gap between the blooper and the spinnaker. Care

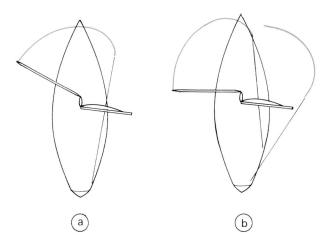

15. *Blooper Trim 2.* In (a) the pole is forward to keep the spinnaker over the centreline of the boat. When the blooper is added, as in (b), the pole is trimmed aft to open the gap between the two sails.

must be taken that the sail does not touch the water; if it were to be caught by the sea it could be sucked under the boat. It will be found that more attention has to be given to adjustment of the halyard than the sheet. If possible, two people should attend to trim, one on the sheet and the other on the halyard. They should place themselves close together so that they are able to communicate and work as a team to keep the sail at its most efficient.

In some conditions it is often found difficult to make the blooper stand properly as it is blanketed by the mainsail. The blooper is so much larger in area than the mainsail that it is important to get it working if conditions are right, even at the expense of the latter. This can be done by partially or completely lowering the mainsail. If the wind is marginally too far aft or slightly too light, it is amazing how much difference it makes to the effectiveness of the blooper if the mainsail is lowered by the equivalent of a reef, or if the clew is let off and pushed a few feet in along the boom. This is a trick I used a lot on my own Three-Quarter-Tonner *Simplicity* where we had a relatively large mainsail. Getting the mainsail out of the way is even more important if a normal genoa or high clewed reacher is being used instead of a specially cut blooper, because the headsail will be almost entirely in the lee of the mainsail (because its luff doesn't sag off to leeward as well as the proper blooper).

Light Weather. In ghosting conditions the blooper is not worth the trouble it takes to keep it full. However, it has more area than the mainsail so, in the lower wind speeds of 5–6 knots, it can sometimes pay to set the blooper and take the mainsail right down; this will allow such wind as there is to get to the bigger sail so that it will set. I recall an occasion some years ago when I was sailing on the Baltic in Kiel Week. We were sent off on the first beat in a light wind and found ourselves fourth boat at the weather mark. On rounding the buoy, the apparent wind dropped almost to nothing as it came astern. We took down our mainsail and, with floater and blooper, *Windlesser* responded well, so that we slowly overhauled the boat ahead who, because of our spread of canvas, could not see what we had done until we drew level with her. She immediately copied us and together we crept up on the next boat. This went on until all four boats were travelling in line abreast. I am glad to tell you that we had been sensible enough to select inside berth, so that we profited from our ploy at the next mark.

Heavy Weather. This is the time to use the blooper to balance the boat as already explained. The sail should be set the moment the spinnaker is up, so that the boat will be easier to control and the spinnaker can be held for longer. If the spinnaker pole is trimmed somewhat further forward than might otherwise seem desirable, the spinnaker will be more in the middle of the boat, thus keeping the sailplan in balance until the blooper is set. The pole may then be trimmed aft again to present more of the sail to the wind, but balanced by the blooper to leeward; see Fig 15. If the next mark requires a gybe and the wind is so strong that spinnaker conditions are marginal, or if the crew is inexperienced, it is not a bad idea to lower the spinnaker before the blooper. Position the boat so that the gybe can be carried out before the buoy is reached, lower the spinnaker and then gybe. The blooper may be left set to weather and the foredeck is clear to hoist the headsail. Boat speed will fall very little and the gybe will be much more under control.

Lowering. The blooper is normally easy to lower for, if the tack is released from the bow and taken aft close to the mast, the sail will quickly collapse as it is blanketed by the mainsail. The foredeck hand can then gather it in and push it down the forehatch. In strong winds, it will empty of wind more quickly if the head of the sail is first raised slightly and the sheet eased; the spinnaker pole may then be allowed to go forward slightly to bring the spinnaker more into the middle of the boat in the interests of keeping imbalance to a minimum as suggested above. When the sail is down, the halyard will have to be passed over the spinnaker sheet to bring it back inside. The sail has to be taken down and re-set when gybing from one spinnaker run to another, and failure to sort out the halyard in this manner will cause problems later.